HOSTAGE

HOSTAGE

A MEMOIR OF TERRORISM, TRAUMA, AND RESILIENCE

Mimi Nichter

Potomac Books | *An imprint of the University of Nebraska Press*

© 2026 by Mimi Nichter

All rights reserved. Potomac Books is an imprint of the University of Nebraska Press.
Manufactured in the United States of America.

For customers in the EU with safety/GPSR concerns, contact:
gpsr@mare-nostrum.co.uk
Mare Nostrum Group BV
Mauritskade 21D
1091 GC Amsterdam
The Netherlands

Library of Congress Control Number: 2025023100

Set in Adobe Text Pro by A. Shahan.

For Mark and our family,
with love and dreams of adventures yet to come

Life can only be understood backwards, but it must be lived forwards.

—SØREN KIERKEGAARD

The wound is the place where the light enters you.

—RUMI

Contents

Illustrations

Author's Note

To reconstruct an event that occurred over fifty years ago, I pored over my journal entries written in the weeks and months following my release and perused newspaper and magazine accounts from that time. Although in my professional life as a cultural anthropologist I rely heavily on interviewing others, for this book, I chose to draw largely from my own memories. Any errors or inconsistencies of the events reported are my own. In most cases, I have changed people's names and identifying details to respect and protect the privacy of these individuals. In several instances I refer to myself with my maiden name, Mimi Beeber. In some cases, the timeline of events and other information has been slightly altered for the sake of narrative flow.

Introduction

During the five decades that have passed since I was a hijack hostage in Jordan, I've rarely talked about the experience except to my closest friends. Even then, I would not tell the story in its entirety but would recount a shortened version, merely sharing that at age twenty I was on a hijacked plane and kept as a hostage. I didn't talk about the bombing of Amman during the civil war, or how close I came to death. I left out the scary parts. When people asked about the hijackers, I mentioned the name of the group—the Popular Front for the Liberation of Palestine—but didn't explain anything about who they were or what they wanted.

Even talking in this truncated way was difficult. No listener response seemed appropriate; either the person felt sorry for me or thought the story was amazing and wanted to hear more. Afterward, I inevitably found myself reliving the hijacking. My head ached and my breath shortened, and for hours or even days afterward, I felt drained and saddened. Not telling the story seemed safer. And the less frequently I told it, the more difficult it became to tell. Within a few years, my secret was sealed. Even in therapy, I focused on current problems and did not mention the hijacking.

In part, my inability and reluctance to tell the story reflected how I had grown up. In my conservative Jewish family, we shared little about our private lives with others. This was certainly not true for all Jewish families, but in our household, we didn't talk about feelings. Whatever was outside the fuzzy boundaries of normal, I learned, was best hidden.

In the immediate aftermath of the ordeal, when I returned to college shortly after my release, I felt untethered from my friends who, like me, were anti–Vietnam War activists. Some of them romanticized my experience with "real revolutionaries" as "far out." Certain that no one could understand what it was like to be held in a war zone, I buried those weeks of my life.

Eventually, I went on to not only survive but thrive, finding my footing as a cultural anthropologist, researching women's health and development in the United States, India, and Indonesia. Focusing on the narratives of young women, I mostly forgot, or at least continued to silence, my own.

I carried on with the story under wraps for decades until a former high school classmate requested an interview about the hijacking. He had become a political scientist and was writing a book on global terrorism. He had recognized my name in newspaper articles about the 1970 hijacking of four airplanes during "Black September."

My first response to his request was to equivocate. It had been years since I had last talked with anyone about the experience. But I was uncomfortable saying no outright, so I said I'd think about it. He had not explained how he would use my story or how he would retell it. What if the interview flung open a door to latent trauma and fear?

Still, my unwillingness to be interviewed felt wrong—selfish, even. Most of my work as an anthropologist depended on people's willingness to speak openly about themselves. How could I refuse to talk about my experience when I depended on others to talk about theirs?

Maybe it was time for me to tell my story.

The following week, as I drove to the interview, my stomach went into full clench. But after sharing a few laughs about high school, I was more at ease. He already knew the details of the hijacking from his research but had many questions. Memories flooded to the surface as I talked about those surreal weeks of my young life; images came to mind quickly, in sharp focus, piling on top of each other like a stack of cards.

Although it was a struggle to find words for an experience I'd long held in silence, over time it slowly became easier to talk about the hijacking with friends. The coping strategy I'd learned as a child, to hide my feelings, no longer served me. In fact, sharing my story provided insight and relief. I started to view myself as a survivor as I read about post-traumatic stress disorder (PTSD) and the lasting impact of trauma on people's lives. These subjects were unexplored in 1970 when the hijacking occurred. Like soldiers returning from combat, we were supposed to adjust, almost as if nothing had happened.

As I found courage in telling the story, the desire to write about the experience emerged periodically. One hot summer day as I was cleaning my home office, I noticed a box with the words "hijacking papers" written in small print. A shiver ran down my spine as I ran my finger over the words. The wide brown tape around the top of the box had lost its stickiness over the years, and the box easily opened.

As I removed the frayed, yellowed papers, I wondered if I had purposefully hidden them to shield myself from the memories within. Or perhaps it had not been important for me to find them until then. Inside was a stack of my handwritten notes from when I first returned home. The box also contained newspaper and magazine articles my parents had collected during the weeks of my captivity.

Each page was covered in crossed-out words and scribbles in the margins, as if even then I had struggled to get the words right. These pages helped me access my earliest reflections on being a hostage. I cried and cried again as I remembered the young college girl I'd been at the time. And yet, despite my sadness, I knew I had stumbled upon something important, a beginning, a pile of memories that could serve as a scaffolding as I built my story word by word.

When I boarded the plane in Tel Aviv on that hot summer morning, I was oblivious to the harm that could occur on a seemingly ordinary flight back to the United States. So were most of, if not all, my fellow passengers. In that pre-9/11 time, few people—particularly a twenty-something like me—had an awareness or understanding of terrorism. It just wasn't on our radar. The age of global terrorism had not yet begun. In contrast, today Americans are inundated with media reports, television specials, and feature-length Hollywood films on hijackings, hostage negotiations, and mass shootings. Terrorism, both domestic and global, is on the rise with ever more terrifying outcomes. Having these images in our minds, we are now primed to anticipate potentially devastating consequences for individuals involved in these types of events.

My hijacking changed the world. There had been hijackings before, but none had been as efficient and bold, and none had focused on the value of hostages as political pawns. Shortly after our return from Jordan, airports around the United States installed metal detectors and conducted searches of people's bodies and their luggage. With a rising awareness of threats among ordinary people, travel would never be the same again.

The Israeli–Palestinian conflict has reached no resolution despite years of attempted negotiation. In fact, it has only escalated. Since the deadly October 7, 2023, attack by Hamas in southern Israel, more than 67,000 Palestinians have been killed by Israeli bombs, and the bodies of thirteen deceased Israeli hostages are still being held in unknown locations around Gaza. This ongoing humanitarian crisis has made this conflict and the history of hostage-taking in the region more important to understand than ever. This book provides a window into a historical event that occurred over fifty years ago. Yet, once again, this regional, and indeed global, conflict is in the forefront of our everyday lives.

For many years, when my husband and I were on vacation and taking long walks along the ocean's edge, I would reflect on the memoir I planned to write someday. But it wasn't until the world shut down for a global pandemic—another pivotal event that would change our lives forever—that I began in earnest. I had retired from teaching at the university, and it was finally time to explore and lay bare my story. With nowhere to go, I journeyed within.

HOSTAGE

PART 1

DAY 1

LEAVING ISRAEL

SEPTEMBER 6, 1970

Sometimes, it pays to be late. I'm the last passenger to board TWA Flight 741 in Tel Aviv. Having barely arrived in time for the 6:00 a.m. departure, I'm put in the only available seat: first class, where I savor the freshly squeezed orange juice and made-to-order omelet, welcome luxuries for my backpacking lifestyle.

Of course, my luck is short-lived.

Within hours, I'll be wishing I'd been a lot later.

After a stop in Frankfurt, I'm moved to an aisle seat in coach. The man beside me is heavyset, his dark hair slicked back and threaded with silver, far from the seatmate I'd hoped for—a handsome twenty-something guy with whom I could flirt and have a drink. After a summer that was a dead loss for romance, I'm ready to get back to my college campus. The constant catcalls and see-through-my-clothes gazes of Israeli men had bothered me, an American student driven abroad by wanderlust. At least at home, guys are a little less obvious about their intentions.

The pilot announces that we're flying over Brussels. Eight hours until we reach New York. I'm trying to read when the air shifts. A woman sprints down the aisle toward the front of the plane, a guy close behind her. I'm unsure how to read the situation—maybe they're having a fight and she's trying to get away from him? Or maybe she's feeling ill and in desperate need of a toilet.

Someone yells, "He's got a gun! She's got a grenade!"

And suddenly, I know exactly how to read it. Or I should know. I hear the words, I understand them, but can't fathom what's happening.

The running man yanks open the blue curtain dividing coach and first class. A stewardess boldly moves from the galley into the aisle in front of him, putting her hands out to block the way. She says something to the man and the woman that I can't make out, but I figure she's telling them they can't go any farther.

The purser, who's been moving through coach selling headphones, rushes down the aisle and taps the man on his shoulder. The man swings around, pointing his gun at him. "Get back, get back! This is a hijack! Hijack!" he shouts. His accent sounds Middle Eastern.

The purser gasps.

Maybe we all gasp. Or maybe we're holding our breaths. It all happens so fast.

The man with the gun steps toward the stewardess. "Imshi, imshi, move it!" he says, motioning her toward the cockpit. His companion follows.

When they reach the cockpit door, the gunman bangs and kicks at it.

The copilot opens the door a crack, and the couple push inside, slamming the door behind them.

The word *hijacking* ripples through the plane like a shock wave. Passengers turn to one another—their partners, family, strangers. I hear the word *grenade* repeated. Painfully aware of how alone I am, I try not to look at anyone. Like a hermit crab, I retreat into myself.

The intercom clicks on from the cockpit, and we hear a new voice—female, with a thick accent. "This is your new captain speaking. You are being taken to a friendly country. Stay calm, we will not harm you. Fasten your seatbelts. Put your hands behind your head."

I'm more confused than panicked. There's no one to ask why we should put our hands behind our heads, although everyone around me is doing it, including the crew. What kind of friendly country wants an airplane full of people? I don't know enough to be afraid. At least, that's what I'm trying to tell myself.

In this era, before the Twin Towers fell, before twenty-four-hour news cycles became the norm, and—perhaps most notably—before any of the things that will follow over the next twenty-one days in my young life, my understanding of what could happen is limited. I vaguely recall that in the 1960s hijackers (or "skyjackers," as they were sometimes called) had diverted planes from the United States to Cuba. Their demands varied. Some of them wanted regular flights to begin between the two countries; others insisted that millions of dollars in ransom be paid. The incidents were, above all, attention grabs. Hijackings typically ended with inconvenience. Passengers were quickly flown back to the United States.

Now that I'm in such a spectacle myself, I want nothing more than to get home, and I'm restless and annoyed. Like other passengers around me,

I quickly remove my hands from my head once we realize the hijackers are not watching us. Despite my lack of information, I'm developing my own theory of what may happen, which helps me feel like I've got control over the situation. I reason that the hijacking will delay our return to New York by a couple of hours, maybe longer. If the hijackers are interested in the plane, they'll want it intact. No bullet holes. And they probably need the pilot, too, so they won't harm him or other crew members. As for the passengers, what would they want with us? Maybe they'll drop us off at some airport, and we'll just have to wait for another plane to fly us back to the States.

I'm pondering this mess when the woman hijacker comes on the intercom with a second announcement. "We're with the Popular Front for the Liberation of Palestine, the PFLP."

I don't follow Middle Eastern politics. I've never heard of this group.

The plane tilts sharply as it changes direction. Bags slide haphazardly under seats into the aisle.

I turn to my seatmate, offering a quick smile. "Hi, I'm Mimi Beeber." I need someone to talk to, and he's older and may understand more of what's going on than I do. So what if he isn't the seatmate I dreamed of, I've got to click into reality here.

"I'm Bob Palumbo," he says. His accent tells me he's a New Yorker, like me. The third person in our row, an elderly man with a blue turban, is seated by the window, fast asleep. He looks like he's from India.

"I couldn't see much, could you?" Bob asks.

I have a better view from my aisle seat, so I describe the couple's dash for the cockpit and the gun in the man's hand, the grenade in hers. "Any ideas about what's going on?"

"We may be heading to Algeria. It felt like the plane was turning south," Bob says. His voice is deep, his tone definitive. "Algerian diplomats are being held in an Israeli prison. Maybe the Palestinians want a prisoner exchange."

I'm impressed by Bob's knowledge of the region. I try to take comfort that, as far as I can tell, he doesn't look worried about getting rerouted to North Africa. Maybe his attitude will rub off on me.

"Wow, sounds complicated.," I say, slumping in my seat. "I hope they don't keep us long. I need to get home. I'm moving back to DC in a couple days to start my senior year at George Washington University."

I take out the TWA magazine from the seat pocket and turn to the world maps on the back pages. Studying them and figuring out how far we are from Algeria provides a momentary distraction.

The first-class cabin is visible, the curtain still open. The male hijacker is pacing the aisle now, wearing a black suit and a white shirt. His hands are on his hips, a cigarette dangling from his lips. His black hair is closely cropped, and he's got a slim build.

His face squeezes into a mean scowl as he points his gun at another stewardess. "Empty first class now! Move people into coach," he snarls.

The stewardess scouts the plane. The flight is full. I don't count, but I'll later learn there are 145 passengers on board. She moves hesitantly down the aisle, assessing where she can possibly relocate the people from the front of the cabin. Before long, fourteen first-class passengers are squeezed into coach seats, each one becoming a fourth person in a three-seat row. The stewardess selects rows with one parent and two children—the only places that can fit an extra person. To get a few more inches of space, she removes the armrests and slips them under the seats. Thankfully, our row is not selected. I'm uncomfortable enough as it is.

Another stewardess passes out earphones—this time for free—so we can distract ourselves with music. This seems confirmation that there is no need for panic—otherwise, wouldn't we need to keep our ears tuned, our eyes peeled? Our flight was scheduled to show a Lee Marvin movie, *Paint Your Wagon*, but the hijacker who has so abruptly taken charge wouldn't allow them to lower the screens, insisting he needs an unobstructed view of the passengers. I'm disappointed; a musical comedy could have helped with my restlessness.

A couple of older people keep heading to the lavatories in the rear of the plane. Maybe it's nerves. There's not much we can do but wait and see where they take us. It seems like even the most alarmed passengers have calmed down since our plane changed course. Perhaps they share my belief that no harm will come to us. Or maybe I'm just oblivious to their tension. The man behind me complains to the person across the aisle that his wife is not carrying her medicine with her, and any delay can be life-threatening. Others voice similar problems.

The cabin crew tries to maintain some sense of regularity on the flight by serving meals from the food cart and offering whiskey or wine for free.

I'm not hungry but decide to eat. Who knows when the next meal will be or what it will be? I'd prefer comfort food, like a bag of pretzels I can pick the salt from, but I take what they're offering.

Many passengers have requested special kosher meals. I grew up in a kosher household, but my older sister and I abandoned those rules years back, indulging in spareribs at Chinese restaurants whenever our parents were out of town. In college, I'd discovered BLT sandwiches, now my favorite lunch.

Bettie, the stewardess serving the meal, looks five years older than me. Tall and slender with pink lipstick, matching nail polish, and false eyelashes, she exudes elegance. I'm an au naturelle type, a hippie, and don't bother with makeup or nail polish. My curly red hair is parted in the middle and reaches halfway down my back. My green cotton minidress is wrinkled.

"Seafood Newburg or beef goulash?" Bettie asks. I'm not sure what either of those are but select the fish. "Do you know where we're going?" I ask as Bettie hands me the lunch plate and a glass of wine. I'm ready for the whole bottle.

"I have no information. It's best if you stay in your seat and keep calm."

The red wine lifts my spirits. "Where'd you get on the plane?" I ask Bob, more inclined to get to know him now.

"Bombay. I travel to India a couple of times a year to buy spices for an import company. The guy next to me boarded there, too. He doesn't speak English."

"Oh, India is on my travel list! My neighbor in Brooklyn is in the Peace Corps, and I've read the letters he sends to his parents. It's a different world." I picture myself on the stoop of our brick house reading Steven's blue aerograms, full of descriptions of life in the Punjab. What wouldn't I give to be there now. Anywhere but here, headed who-knows-where.

"Earlier today I got off the plane in Tel Aviv, where they make you go through security and immigration even if you're getting back on a plane," Bob says. "I've got a lot of arrival and departure stamps in my passport. I collect them—it's sort of my hobby. I've got a few from Israel even though I never spent a night there."

"That's cool," I say. But his talk about detours has only reminded me of the one we're currently on. "I hope we land in the next hour or two," I venture. I'm still thinking we'll be late getting to New York, but nothing bad will happen. But it would be nice to hear him say it.

"Let's wait and see. Anyway, there's nothing we can do," Bob says. His calm demeanor helps.

I walk to the toilet, where there's a short line. In the back galley, a group of ultra-Orthodox Jewish men in long black jackets and hats are bowing and reciting Hebrew prayers in hushed voices, small prayer books in their hands.

I hope someone is listening to their prayers. As for me, I'm not really the praying type anymore.

From age six to twelve, I attended an Orthodox Jewish yeshiva. We studied Hebrew religious texts all morning and had English classes in the afternoon. Girls and boys sat on different sides of the room and played separately during recess, which we had on the roof. My family belonged to a Conservative temple, where men and women sat and prayed together. I felt different from my classmates; if asked what synagogue our family belonged to, I didn't answer. Telling the name of our temple was a dead giveaway that we weren't religious enough.

My mother has always been adamant that my older sister, Debi, and I never discuss our family life with others. We're not supposed to tell people that our parents work in Philadelphia, leaving Debi and me alone in the house in Brooklyn three days a week while our mother joins our father to work in his medical supply business. Or that my older brother has delusions and talks to people who aren't there. Or that my father comes home only on weekends. Even when he's in town, he spends his time at the temple attending services, watching baseball, or napping on the couch. I'm pretty sure he doesn't know me since he always calls me Debi.

Now, as I walk back from the bathroom, I look around the plane, struck by how different I am from the many modestly dressed religious passengers. Settling back into my seat, I think about my summer in Israel, picking pears on a kibbutz. I convinced my parents to pay for my travel by telling them that spending time on a communal farm would help me experience what it meant to be Jewish. They hoped I'd return home an observant Jew, like them.

The truth was, I never had any such intention. I'd learned all I wanted to know about Judaism by the time I was twelve, and after studying in London during my junior year, I'd itched to travel again as soon as

FIG. 1. This photo was taken during Mimi Nichter's semester abroad in England, six months before the hijacking. Author's collection.

possible. Life in London, and my low-cost jaunts to Scotland, France, and Morocco, had opened a world wider than Brooklyn. I was eager to explore, and Israel was a stop on my global travel path. A stop I correctly calculated that my parents would approve of.

On my days off work, I'd traveled around Israel with friends from the kibbutz, mostly other foreigners. The country was small enough that I was also comfortable venturing alone, hitchhiking when I could. I spoke and read Hebrew and, though far from fluent, I enjoyed expressing myself in the nuances of a different language and wasn't shy in speaking.

Lost in the memories, I doze and awake to another announcement from the female hijacker. The sun is setting so I must have been asleep for a few hours. My ability to sleep soundly despite where I find myself is the best trait I inherited from my family.

"We'll be landing soon in Jordan. It's a friendly country," the hijacker says.

The pilot flies in circles for at least thirty minutes.

"I guess we didn't fly to Algeria, huh?" I say to Bob. "I don't think of Jordan as a friendly country for people coming from Israel."

He strains to peer out the window over the Indian guy and confirms that he doesn't see a runway or anything resembling an airport. No tower, no terminal. "Maybe the pilot's looking for a safe place to land. It's dark out there. All I can see are some flickering flames on the ground."

I'm feeling nauseated from all the circling and grab the white paper barf bag from the seat pocket, hoping I won't need it.

"Take slow, deep breaths," Bob instructs. "It helps."

The deep breathing calms my nausea, but I'm getting worried about what will happen once we land. The "fasten seatbelt" light comes on.

"Prepare for a crash landing," the pilot announces. "Fold forward towards your knees and rest your head there. Place your hands around your legs."

If my worry level was a pale yellow before, it's now flashing red.

I follow the pilot's instructions. The plane touches down, taxies a short distance, and comes to a hard stop. The pilot has managed a safe and smooth landing, like we were at a real airport.

The Indian man by the window, jolted awake, utters his first two words. "New York?"

DAY 1

LANDING AT GUNPOINT

From my aisle seat, I peer across our newly awakened seatmate, who is about to be sorely disappointed. It's dark outside. Torches stuck in oil barrels are the only lights that line the makeshift runway. This is far from New York's bustling terminals—it isn't even an airport. Headlights of cars and trucks parked in the distance are directed at the plane, casting an eerie glow. Maybe that's why the pilot kept circling, making sure he'd be able to bring the plane down in this remote location.

Within moments, the hijackers open the forward door. A wooden ladder perched on a pickup truck is thrust against the side of the plane, and the couple descend. An exuberant crowd has gathered on the desert floor, cheering wildly at the arrival of an American aircraft. There are lots of men in khaki uniforms, their heads wrapped in scarves, only their eyes visible. Most have rifles slung over their shoulders.

Inside the cabin, we wait in silence, holding our collective breaths. With the engines off, there's no electricity—no lights, no air conditioning. The hot air is still. Passengers are lighting up cigarettes and the smoke is circulating, a toxic heaviness filling the plane. There's a smoking section in the rear, but we seem to have abandoned any pretense of rules. Curtains no longer divide any of the cabins anyway.

I stare at the alarming spectacle outside. I saw plenty of soldiers in Israel, but they didn't surround me or seem threatening. This is different. With all those guns, are they planning to shoot us?

"Wow, they're freaking out down there." My trembling voice sounds unfamiliar, like it's coming from somebody else's mouth.

"Our hijackers brought a packed plane to the middle of nowhere." Bob's voice is calm, but his furrowed brow reveals worry. "These soldiers . . . commandos . . . have a lot of hostages now. Who knows what they have planned for us."

Hostages. I don't like the sound of that word.

After a few moments, a new woman climbs aboard and stands in front of the economy cabin. With the crowd of men outside, I'm surprised to see another woman who seems to be in charge and relieved she doesn't have a gun. She's wearing green army fatigues, and her hair is covered by a tightly wrapped black-checked kaffiyeh, a symbol of resistance and solidarity worn by Palestinians in Israel and around the Middle East. I almost bought one of those scarves in the Jerusalem market for my roommate who—like me—was a member of a left-wing student activist group back in the United States.

"We're passing out landing cards," she says in English. "Fill them out completely with your name, address, passport number, and nationality. In ten minutes, we'll collect these with your passports."

I take a deep breath, hoping to calm the pounding in my chest. All around, passengers are talking, an uneasy familiarity developing.

Across the aisle, a woman and her husband search her purse and remove two Israeli and two U.S. passports. They seem ultra-Orthodox; she's wearing an auburn wig, a navy-blue long-sleeved blouse, and a matching skirt that covers her calves. His full silver beard covers his upper chest, and he wears a baggy black jacket and a tall black hat. I stare in amazement as the husband frantically rips the Israeli passports while the wife snips the covers with nail scissors she took from her bag. They stuff the larger bits into motion sickness bags, put small pieces of the identification pages into their mouths, and swallow them, gulping water to wash the pieces down. The woman shoves the airsick bags far down in the crevices between their seats.

I turn and see Bob is also watching. "What's that about?" I whisper.

"If our captors find out they have Israeli *and* U.S. passports, they could be in a lot of trouble," he whispers back.

I know some people hold dual Israeli and U.S. citizenship. An Israeli passport makes it obvious a person is Jewish, but how would the hijackers know about the rest of us? Are they interested in our citizenship, our religion, or both? People often say my red hair and freckles "don't look Jewish." I think they mean it as a compliment, but it doesn't feel like one. Jews have lived for centuries in many parts of the world, and there are many ways of being and looking Jewish. Implying otherwise enforces a harmful stereotype, even if I don't fit the bill.

There are many ultra-Orthodox Jews on the plane, along with Modern Orthodox Jews, who wear regular clothes and are largely distinguished by the men's skullcaps. Fearing repercussions for their religion, many men remove their head coverings. Women remove necklaces with Jewish stars or the Hebrew character for life, *chai*. I'm wearing a Jewish star, too, and, seeing what others are doing, I hurriedly remove mine and put it in my dress pocket. When my aunt and uncle in Tel Aviv gave me the necklace as a gift, they said they hoped wearing it would remind me I always had a home to return to in Israel. I feel guilty taking it off but can't risk what it might mean to keep it on.

The woman commando collects our passports and the forms with personal information and leaves the plane, climbing down the ladder. I'm uneasy and wonder if I'll see my passport again and how I'll reenter the United States without it. I imagine myself languishing for hours at JFK airport while immigration officials sort out this mess.

A brooding silence descends again on the plane as we consider the potential dangers of the new terrain. Within a half hour, more Palestinians come on board, strolling down the aisle, staring and glaring. Most wear khaki shirts, combat pants, and boots. Some have black berets, others have kaffiyehs tied around their heads. Most carry rifles. A young man walks by me, his eyes focused on my bare legs. Scrawny with black hair and a pencil-thin mustache, he looks like he can't be more than fifteen. My aisle seat is doing nothing to disguise my minidress, an unfortunate clothing choice grabbed in a hurry that morning. I look down to avoid his gaze and shudder when another soldier saunters down the aisle, his rifle brushing my arm.

After their deliberately menacing walk through the plane, most of the commandos descend the ladder, but two remain, standing guard with their guns by the front exit.

I always feel edgy at the end of a long flight, wanting to stand and walk quickly to get the kinks out of my legs and get the blood flowing again. Now, the sensation is amplified. Everything is amplified. The smoky air is thick, and it's hard to breathe. People continue to light up wherever they're seated, as it might help them relax.

It's dawning on me—maybe more slowly than others—that the situation is far more serious than I presumed. The excitement of the Palestinians outside and the parade of armed guerrillas inside does not bode well for our quick release. My vulnerability as a young woman traveling alone is coming into sharp focus.

Soon afterward, we hear a deafening sound from behind our plane, so loud that I can no longer hear my thoughts. I turn to Bob, who has become my default go-to person as it becomes harder to face this unfolding crisis alone. There's something friendly and unassuming about him.

"Now what?" I ask, craning my neck toward the window.

A nearby passenger screams, raw panic in her voice. "Another plane . . . huge fireballs . . . coming our way!"

"We're going up in flames!" a woman cries out.

I can't see what they're talking about, which is probably for the best, but their frantic outbursts tell me there's no escape. We're trapped.

Just then, the flight engineer, Al, leaves the cockpit and moves to the front of the coach cabin, a bullhorn in hand. "Listen up! Don't worry! Another plane, Swissair, was hijacked and our Captain Woods helped them land. Their pilot put his engines into reverse to avoid ramming us. Sand got into the engines and caused those fireballs. We're safe . . . don't panic. Everybody, please, stay in your seats."

Despite Al's attempts to calm us, Bob and I hear from other passengers who could see out the window that the Swissair jet came within a hundred feet of our plane. It's miraculous their pilot averted a collision.

"A second hijacked plane . . ." Bob's voice cracks as he meets my eyes. "I sure hope there's safety in numbers." Shiny beads of sweat cover his forehead, some sliding down his cheeks. His calm facade, like mine, is dissolving.

What I don't know yet is that in the space of three hours, the Popular Front for the Liberation of Palestine has attempted to hijack four planes with more than six hundred passengers and crew combined. Two are from the largest American airlines, Pan American and our Trans World Airlines flight; the others are the Swissair plane now beside us and an El Al flight.

Fifteen minutes after we departed Frankfurt, there was an attempted hijacking of an El Al flight from Tel Aviv to New York, which was foiled by airplane security on board, who killed the male hijacker. Passengers restrained the second hijacker, Leila Khaled, a twenty-four-year-old

Palestinian woman, with neckties and scarves. When the plane landed in London, Khaled was arrested by British police.

At the same time, a Pan Am jumbo jet headed to New York from Amsterdam was also hijacked by the Popular Front and redirected to Beirut's airport, which was not equipped to safely land such a large plane, but the hijackers insisted. As soon as the plane landed, commandos rushed on board with suitcases full of grenades and explosives. They ordered the pilot to fly to Cairo and, after takeoff, wired the plane. As the plane touched down at Cairo airport, they lit the fuses and announced the plane would explode in minutes. The pilots released the evacuation slides, and passengers, crew, and guerrillas slid down, escaping moments before the plane blew up. Some passengers were injured, but no one died. The guerrillas were taken into custody by Egyptian police.

Our TWA flight was targeted as a symbol of the United States, whom the Palestinians perceived as the leader of international imperialism. A few months before our hijacking, a Popular Front spokesperson had declared at a press conference: "By supplying Israel with huge quantities of aid, America is responsible for keeping the Palestinian people homeless and living in tents for over twenty-two years under the shadow of hunger and disease." He'd gone on to say, "TWA flights to Israel brought visitors and tourists to enemies of the Palestinians who are occupying our land by force."

In other words, my fellow TWA passengers and I had picked the wrong flight that day.

Minutes later, a stately Arab doctor wearing a navy suit, white starched shirt, and wide striped tie boards the plane. A crew member introduces him. "This is a representative from the Red Crescent with some announcements for us."

I've never heard of the Red Crescent but gather it's an Arab version of the Red Cross, like the Israelis' Magen David Adom, literally the Red Star of David.

Despite his limited English, we understand we'll be staying on the plane for a day or two. He reassures us not to be afraid and promises to return in the morning with more news. We have no opportunity to ask questions.

Stay on the plane for a day or two? We're going to sleep here, sitting up, all night? The plane already reeks of cigarette smoke, dirty diapers, smelly socks, and sweaty armpits. Mothers complain they need milk and food for their crying babies. Some adults are insisting they need medicines in their checked luggage.

I close my eyes and imagine my mother and father waiting for me at JFK airport, anxiously checking the arrival board, walking to the gate, wondering why the flight has not yet arrived.

DAY 2

OVERNIGHT ON THE PLANE

Sleep comes in fragments. My bra digs into my skin, and it's hard to get comfortable sitting upright. So much for my ability to sleep anywhere. When I awake, the sun is rising. Out the window, the desert floor appears sun-cracked and scorched. In the distance, Bedouin herders in long robes follow their camels, their heads turning toward the two massive airplanes out of place in the otherwise barren landscape. Some herders ride their camels across the desert. There are no roads. Men are digging trenches in the sand and aiming guns at the planes.

I'm alarmed. Are they digging mass graves for us? Why else would they need those trenches? Later, we'd learn that the PFLP were preparing to fight off a possible rescue attempt by the Jordanian army, who'd been alerted to our situation.

An unfamiliar flag planted in the sand waves gently beside an open-sided tent. The flag has three horizontal stripes—black, white, and green—overlaid with a red triangle coming from the hoist. A group of khaki-clad men sit on a carpet in the tent. Eight dusty pickup trucks and jeeps are parked on the sand near the plane. Perhaps a quarter of a mile away, tanks in a semicircular formation point their artillery at us.

During the night, the temperature drops, and I shiver from cold and fear. The few available blankets have been given to children and the elderly, the crew apologetically explaining that daytime flights do not stock many blankets. I have an Israeli army shirt in my backpack but, given the bizarre shredding and eating of passports by those sitting near me, it seems too risky to put it on. The shirt was a farewell gift from my Israeli friend Ari, who'd recently completed his compulsory military service. It occurs to me that I should probably get rid of the shirt but can't see how. Obviously, I can't swallow it or shove it between the seats like my neighbors did with their passports.

I wiggle and squirm in my narrow seat. There's so much to worry about. What should I say if the hijackers ask about my religion? During the Holocaust some Jews tried, usually unsuccessfully, to conceal their identity. I don't like the idea of lying, but what if it could save my life? I know no one on the plane. Perhaps I can simply pretend I'm not Jewish.

After a short while, I extinguish that line of thought, like a cigarette that's reached the filter. Despite my difficulties with organized religion at home, the summer in Israel has led me to a new cultural identity, one not dependent on how often I go to synagogue or how observant I am. I've discovered I can be secular and still be a Jew. If I renounced that under pressure, what kind of a person would that make me?

Away from these swirling thoughts, I'm aware my foot has fallen asleep, and it stings with pins and needles. I walk to the toilet, hoping movement will help, and join the line of passengers waiting for the three lavatories in the economy section. I hope there will be water in the sink so I can wash my hands and face. I don't have a toothbrush or toothpaste in my hastily packed carry-on. In an unlikely stroke of luck, I'm wearing my tortoiseshell eyeglasses, not my contact lenses, something I rarely do as I'm self-conscious about how I look in specs.

I was a mess when I boarded the plane in Tel Aviv. Typically a sound sleeper, I'd overslept for our ridiculously early morning departure. My green minidress had been lying on the floor next to the bed, so I'd thrown it on. I would have done a lot of things differently if I'd ever imagined I would still be wearing it twenty-four hours later with access only to the things in my backpack. Now, I'm wishing again I'd missed the flight.

A twenty-something guy with long wavy brown hair waits ahead of me in line. "I'm Mike," he offers. He's tall with an athletic build and an easy smile. "How ya holding up? Get much sleep?"

"I'm Mimi. Not much sleep—I just couldn't get comfortable." I notice his bell-bottom jeans and faded T-shirt and imagine he might be an American college student like I am. "Heard anything about what's going on or where we are?"

"I heard from one of the crew that we're ten miles from Zarqa, which is about twenty miles from Amman. We're in the north of Jordan, fifteen miles from the nearest road, and fifty miles from Israel."

FIG. 2. The plane was redirected to a remote desert region in Jordan, about twenty miles north of Amman. Central Intelligence Agency photo.

I shake my head in disbelief, a wave of frustration washing over me. "A whole day of flying and I'm about where I started," I say. "What is this place anyway? It's like a big desolate nothing."

"Yeah, I know," Mike says, running his hand through his hair. "We're on an old airstrip called Dawson's Field—named after Sir Walter Dawson, a British Royal Air Force officer who trained pilots here during World War II. Our kidnappers are calling it Revolution Airport."

I roll my eyes. "It doesn't look like any airport I've been to, that's for sure."

"It's not, really. I mean, there's no concrete runway or anything, it's just hardened sand. That's why it took the pilot so long to land. He didn't know what he was landing on. A heavy plane like this could just sink on soft sand. I heard he was dumping fuel when we were circling so the plane would be lighter."

My foot is still tingling, so I shake it and wiggle my toes. It feels almost good to have such an ordinary problem, something in my body that I can focus on. I'm trying not to think about those trenches outside. "They'd better send us home today," I say. "Can't take another night on the plane."

Mike nods. "I'm ready to get home too—start my junior year at the University of Wisconsin next week."

A woman and her toddler leave the toilet and Mike rushes in. I guess he needs to pee as much as I do. I glance into the galley. Mary, a brunette stewardess, is washing baby bottles and filling them with milk. Behind her, another stewardess arranges bread rolls on a food cart. I'm suddenly hungry.

The lavatory door opens, but my happiness ends there. Inside I see that the bowl is backed up, the stench of urine wafts in the air, and paper towels are strewn on the floor. Holding my breath, using my hand to mask my nose and mouth, I relieve myself, but the toilet doesn't flush, and no water comes from the tap. Fearing the toilet paper will soon run out, I stuff some in my pocket and get out fast.

Many passengers are walking up and down the aisles to stretch their legs. The two armed Palestinians at the front door watch their movements unflinchingly. I'm not sure why they're bothering to monitor us; it's not as if we can go anywhere. About 8:00 a.m., our captors bring breakfast on board, which is distributed by Mary and Bettie. We each receive a plastic bag containing one-half of a pita bread, a small piece of sheep-milk cheese, and a hard-boiled egg stamped with *Bulgaria,* which I guess is the country of its origin. Lukewarm sweetened tea is served in flimsy white plastic cups, which we are instructed to keep for future use.

"When are we getting off this plane?" the burly man in the seat behind me barks. "My wife's diabetic and she's almost out of medicine." This is the fourth time I've heard him complain about her health problem, and his level of worry is increasing with each passing hour. Through the space

FIG. 3. On the first morning in Jordan, the view out the window revealed a vast barren desert with no roads in sight. From the PBS American Experience video *Hijacked* (2006).

between the seats, I've heard his wife say she's feeling weak. I noticed her husband had to help her when she went to the bathroom.

"I'll let the people know about her health condition," the stewardess says flatly. "I'll get back to you once I'm through with the service."

"You better," he growls. "I'm not gonna sit by while she gets sick. I don't know what these Palestinians want with us, but I do know my wife can't go hours without food or water. When she runs out of medicine, she could go into shock."

A young mother traveling alone with her infant motions to Bettie. "What do these hijackers really want?" she pleads, bobbing her baby up and down on her knee. "We can't sit like this much longer."

Bettie rests her hand gently on the woman's shoulder, damp from baby dribble. "Let's hope they'll let us go soon."

I cannot imagine sitting in a narrow seat with a chubby, drooling baby on my lap. How is she changing his diaper? Not often enough judging by the pungent odor emanating from her seat. There isn't much room on the floor, and there is no light in the toilet. The baby's high-pitched wailing grates on my nerves and probably on others' nerves, too. Still, I feel sorry for the mother—and all the mothers—as there is little they can do to comfort the little ones.

Mary and Bettie distribute white cloth napkins from the first-class cabin to mothers who have exhausted the diapers they brought on board. Restless children dash down the aisles despite their parents' efforts to confine them to their seats. A head count is impossible, but the crying and shrieking leads me to believe there are at least ten infants and toddlers on board, and an additional twenty children between the ages of five and fifteen. Someone said there were four children—as young as eight—traveling alone. If I feel isolated and utterly lost at more than twice their age, I can't begin to imagine how they must feel. Maybe I can offer to help; even talking to the kids who are on their own could be useful to them. Having someone older to turn to, like Bob, has made me feel better.

I haven't thought about the width of a plane before, but now I'm bothered by how little space is available. The plane is probably less than twelve feet across, with three seats on either side of the aisle. Even though I've gotten out of my seat a few times, my legs are still cramped and my lower back aches.

As the sun moves higher, the plane quickly goes from uncomfortably cold to unbearably hot, and with the engines still turned off, there is no air conditioning. It must be 120 degrees in here. My bra is damp with sweat, and moisture is collecting around the backs of my knees. Sweat droplets gather on my forehead, some falling onto my eyelids. Even my neck feels wet, like it's a lawn of morning dewdrops. *Gross.* I have never been a person who sweats much, so all this dripping is freaking me out. My hair, damp with the hot air, sticks to my neck. I put it in a braid, a slight improvement, and use the plastic safety card from the seat pocket as a fan.

Most passengers close the window shades to block the unrelenting sun. Crew members release the emergency doors over the wings by pressing the unlatch button, pulling the doors inward, and removing them. It requires two crew members to lift them and, after they come off, they carry them to the front of the plane. It brings some air inside but doesn't cool us off.

The commandos allow us to walk in the aisle and visit other passengers periodically, but one of the PFLP members gets angry when too many people are out of their seats. Keeping us seated is a method of control.

"SIT DOWN, NOW!" he booms. He has an automatic rifle over his shoulder but wears khaki slacks and a striped men's dress shirt, like he's come from an office. Bassam, as I hear others call him, has an authoritative air and an excellent command of English.

"Stay seated," he says. "If you need to go to the bathroom, raise your hand. We'll take you one at a time."

I turn to Bob. "Now what? They're going to treat us like we're in kindergarten?"

"It's probably just a momentary thing," Bob says, squeezing his pudgy hands into fists and releasing them. I notice he's wearing a wedding band, and I wonder if he's got kids. "We've got bigger things to worry about."

Throughout the morning, a stream of Palestinian guerrillas and other men and women climb the ladder into the plane. They saunter down the aisle, savoring their catch as if we were big fish who would garner a good price at market. I stare at them, too, curious about who they are. Some men are wearing camouflage shirts and pants, others wear blue jeans and tee shirts, and others are in long white robes, their heads swathed in black-and-white checked kaffiyehs. Some female commandos are dressed in long-sleeved gray shirts and matching pants, which I think may be the women's uniform of the PFLP. Some wear hijabs or loose head coverings.

Each time they stroll down the aisle, a jolt of fear courses through my body. I wish I were invisible so I could hide from their glares. Our flight's copilot seems to have appointed himself to advocate for those on board. We know his name is Jim Majer—all the crew wear name tags—and he's a tall, handsome, kindhearted man who observes how their guns are frightening us. I overhear him speaking to Bassam, requesting that the parade of Palestinians be stopped. If guns must be on the plane, Jim reasons, can't they please be restricted to those standing guard by the front exit? Look at how cooperative we are all being, after all.

Miraculously, it works. Within hours, there are fewer unwelcome guests on board. "Hey, I feel like we have more breathing room now," I comment to Bob. "It's just us passengers again."

"Yeah, and there's more news," he whispers. "An older woman a few rows back has a small radio. Her name's Hannah. She knows Arabic and has been listening to a local station. They announced that two planes were hijacked to the desert! Hannah's keeping the radio hidden so the guerrillas won't take it."

"Do you think people in the U.S. have heard yet? I'm wondering if my parents have any idea what's happened." When I was at college, I was rarely anxious to go home, but now my thoughts repeatedly turn to my family.

"I bet the U.S. government knows the plane's been hijacked," Bob replies. During our time on the ground, his jowly face has kept changing from engaged to distant. The tension of the situation, not knowing what will happen next, is getting to all of us. "The leader of the Jordanian army is in that tent, talking with the Palestinians. I heard he's trying to get us released. It's a good sign that some negotiation is going on."

"I guess Bassam is in the tent, too. He's the guy who seems to be in charge," I say.

"Bassam? You're on a first name basis with these guys?" Bob chuckles.

"I'm good with names, but clueless with history. Can you explain what's going on now?" I don't usually like to reveal my ignorance but, given the situation, it hardly matters.

"The king of Jordan—King Hussein—and his military don't want us here. They're angry that the Palestinians have hijacked these planes," Bob explains. "We're not *their* hostages, we're hostages of the Popular Front for the Liberation of Palestine, who are refugees in this country."

We are in the middle of a complicated political situation, and the negotiations yield some results. In the afternoon, Bassam announces the release of those passengers who are citizens of India, France, Greece, and a few other European countries. Those to be freed are to come to the front of the plane carrying their hand luggage. Bob nudges the Indian man to pick up his bag and walk forward. A minibus with the International Red Cross insignia is parked near the airplane, waiting for them. I note that it's a different organization than the local Red Crescent.

We watch in envy as thirty lucky passengers disembark from the TWA and Swissair planes and board the bus. Once that group has cleared, Bassam calls a second group—women with young children and children traveling alone. In a frenzy, this group pack up their hand luggage and move to the exit. Orthodox women move slowly down the aisle balancing infants and luggage, three or four children straggling behind. Some women sob as they leave their husbands sitting on the plane. I barely restrain my own tears, devastated I can't get off the plane with them.

Bassam and a few other guerrillas huddle together, having a discussion in first class. Something has changed, and they now call *all* the women off the plane. With a surge of adrenaline bordering on hope, I grab my two small backpacks from the overhead compartment, say a swift goodbye to Bob, and head down the aisle.

Bassam and a female comrade in khakis stand by the exit door in the first-class cabin. He addresses her as Halla, and she seems to be following his lead.

As each woman and her family approaches the open door, we are asked our name, nationality, and religion. It seems most of the Jewish women are saying they are Jews, but I have no idea who is telling the truth.

When asked her religion, a teenage girl in front of me, Carol, replies, "Why do you want to know? What difference does it make?" I'm surprised she is challenging Bassam; it seems risky.

Bassam looks at her intently. "Oh, you're Jewish." His voice is gruff.

"No, I'm Protestant," she replies. He waves her on, and she gets off the plane. Carol and I talked earlier in the day; she is a high school senior from Scarsdale traveling with two girlfriends. The girls spent time together in Israel on a kibbutz.

Bassam looks directly at me. The intensity of his glare is chilling. "Name, nationality?" His questions are simple and anticipated but pierce me like darts. The uncertainty stretches the moment in the desert heat.

The muscles in my throat tighten, and I struggle to answer. I turn my gaze downward. My voice quavers. "Mimi Beeber, American."

He jots my response on his clipboard and shoots his next question at me, the one I've been dreading, "Religion?"

My heart hammers. He probably hears it. I'm no closer to guessing what will happen if I answer honestly—but my conviction has solidified. Having been raised in a religious family, I can't lie. And even if I could, I'm not about to let go of my new secular Jewish identity.

"I'm Jewish," I say, trying to steady my voice.

Bassam instructs me to get off the plane.

Climbing down is not easy, especially for women with babies and luggage in their arms. A rickety wooden ladder rests on the back of a pickup truck, and it's a big step down to the top rung. A coarse sisal rope hangs off its side in case we need to hold on for support. The woman who was sitting near me with the shrieking baby prepares to descend. With great difficulty she manages to get down to the first rung clutching her squirmy child, while lugging a diaper bag on one shoulder and a bulging square bag on the other. A commando climbs a few rungs and motions for her to

FIG. 4. The Trans World Airlines (TWA) and Swissair planes are shown at Dawson's Field. The Popular Front for the Liberation of Palestine (PFLP) draped the logo of their group on the door of the plane. *Newsweek*, September 21, 1970.

hand him the baby, who begins bawling at the sight of the unfamiliar man. Refusing to leave his mother's arms, the boy burrows into her shoulder. When I offer to carry the diaper bag, she readily agrees.

Clinging to the ladder with my backpacks and her bag, I quickly realize that the guerrillas on the ground can see up my short dress. Self-conscious, I move quickly and jump off the back of the truck, waving off their offers of assistance.

I join the other women and children who are crammed in with all their belongings on a dusty old minibus. I feel relieved as I settle in, hopeful that our situation is about to change, but we are soon ordered to get back out. One of our captors, Ramy, a husky man with bushy eyebrows and an unkempt mustache, orders us to form a circle on the desert floor. Two other guerrillas enter the center of the circle, their rifles pointed at us. I tremble, glancing again at the freshly dug trenches, fearing we are about to be victims of a firing squad.

It's been a volatile twenty-four hours. I'm quickly learning it's dangerous to make assumptions—including that exiting the plane puts us closer to freedom.

Terrified mothers try unsuccessfully to comfort bawling babies, and young children hide behind their mothers' legs as they bake in the sun. A female PFLP member reads a list of passengers who are to get back on the minibus, presumably, once again, to be released.

We listen intently.

Carol's name is called.

My name is not.

A tear skims my cheek. All the women leaving Revolution Airport are non-Jews. They're directed to a bus marked with a Red Cross insignia and driven away. We have no idea where they are being taken. The Jewish women and children remain on the desert floor, sweltering and despondent. A few non-Jewish women refuse to leave, choosing instead to remain with their husbands, who are still inside the plane.

We are ordered to climb back on the TWA plane, and my heart sinks. Men, women, and children from the Swissair plane are boarding another bus. It looks like they are letting many more passengers leave from that flight. For the first time, I wonder if maybe my bigger issue is that I'm American, but there was no disguising that, either.

As we wait for our turn on the ladder, Irene, a slim woman with pale blue eyes, confides she is an Auschwitz survivor, returning from her first trip to Israel with her two young sons. Fighting back tears, she shares, "The way they've separated us into Jews and non-Jews—I never thought I'd experience this again, but here it is. And earlier today, a German man sitting across from me on the plane called a Palestinian over and told him he wasn't Jewish. He offered him a wad of money to buy his freedom. The soldier laughed and told him to put his cash away. 'We're not thieves. We are fighting for our freedom,' the Palestinian man said. When he moved away, I told the passenger in German, 'This time you'll have to die with the rest of us.'"

Irene's painful past is deeply unsettling, as is our present. We are so close to freedom, yet it is so far away. And it's only been two days—but it seems like a lot more. How can this be happening? I know this thinking is destructive but, at the moment, I'm powerless to control it.

Then it's our turn to climb back on the plane.

All told, thirty-seven people—all non-Jews—have been released from the TWA plane. About one hundred people, including thirty-three children, are left on board. Almost all who remain are Americans and Jewish. With no choice but to obey, I settle back in my seat next to Bob, wiping tears away with the back of my hand. I need to appear strong, like I've got my emotions under control. That's what I've been taught by my mother, to look like it's all okay, even if everything is falling apart. I never questioned why I had to act that way, but this is not the time to analyze my dysfunctional family.

"I'm so sorry you didn't get to go home," Bob says, his voice soft with empathy. "What's going on doesn't make a lot of sense. Lots of the people the PFLP are keeping are Jewish, but not all of them. I'm Italian Catholic, but I guess they saw all those Israeli stamps on my passport and thought I had a connection to the country. My damn hobby! And the crew, the pilot and copilot, and some of the other passengers are not Jewish. They're still onboard."

I relay Irene's story to Bob, and I feel the gut punch of her story all over again. But I feel proud, too, that I didn't lie about being Jewish, even if I'm paying a steep price. And I realize, of course, my experience is nothing like what Irene went through.

After our return, the news would report that the release of non-Jewish passengers had resulted in an outcry by twenty-five Jewish organizations in the United States. The heads of these organizations called on President Nixon to permit "no differentiation" between Jewish and non-Jewish hijack victims and insisted on equal treatment of all passengers. They urged the president to use every tool available to avoid "an Auschwitz in the desert." Two Holocaust survivors living stateside, whose young daughter was traveling alone on our plane, called the CEO of TWA and demanded that the airlines send a plane to Jordan immediately to bring all hostages back to the United States. The airlines explained they could not do that as the PFLP had specifically refused to release Jewish passengers. The PFLP were looking at all Jewish passengers as potential Zionists, individuals who were staunch supporters of the Jewish state of Israel.

Many years later, we'd learn that PFLP doctrine did not discriminate against Jews but did consider Zionists and imperialists to be their enemies. Zionists, from the PFLP perspective, were those who had invaded and stolen their homeland. However, this distinction was not evident to me, or to many other passengers, at the time.

Sitting on the plane after the buses are out of sight, the present makes its own demands. As I wait in line again for the bathroom, I'm standing by a row where a mother sits with her two young daughters. The younger girl looks about seven and has braided red hair and freckles across her nose and cheeks, like me. She's holding a checkerboard and whining, begging her mother to play with her.

"Hi, I'm Mimi," I say. "I see you've got checkers. If you wait till I've gone to the toilet, I'll play a game with you. What's your name?"

"I'm Sharon," she says, turning to her mom for permission to play with a stranger. Her mom nods.

"I'll look for empty seats where we can spread out. Be back soon!" I say, smiling. It feels good to have purpose. Something to do besides worry and wait.

"Can I come too?" the older sister asks. Her straight auburn hair is tied back in a high ponytail. "I'm Margie. I'll bring Mad Libs."

"Great! I love Mad Libs."

"Sounds like fun," a young woman waiting in line nearby says. She has olive skin and straight black hair reaching down her back. "I've got a pack of cards in my bag. Can I join? And there's a little girl sitting across from me. I'll ask her if she wants to play. I'm Rachel."

"I'm Mimi. We can be the official TWA camp counselors." I'm delighted to have someone to help with the kids and who might become a friend.

The two sisters and I settle into an empty row. Rachel returns with two girls, so we now have four kids aged seven to ten. Sitting three on each side of the aisle, we have space for our games. I play checkers with the younger girls, while Rachel teaches the older girls to play gin rummy. The children's laughter floats through the air.

Our fun ends when Ramy, the bushy-browed guard, stops by our row. "All of you, back to your seats, right now," he snaps.

With a hundred people on the plane, our captors seem suspicious of any group activity, even our innocuous games with children.

Across the desert, unbeknownst to us, a Popular Front for the Liberation of Palestine spokesperson in Amman was articulating their first demands to various governments: the release of three guerrillas jailed in Switzerland, three guerrillas held in Germany, the hijacker Leila Khaled in Britain, and an unspecified number of Palestinians held in Israeli prisons. The PFLP had targeted planes from countries where their comrades were held. When Israel agreed to these demands, they would provide the names of those held in their prisons whom they wanted released.

The initial response to these demands would follow the long-standing U.S. policy of not negotiating with terrorists. The secretary of state at the time, William Rogers, described the two sides of this dilemma as either "giving in to fedayeen blackmail" and bringing the hostages home, or not negotiating and running the risk of losing lives. The U.S. policy was based on the belief that meeting the demands of terrorists would encourage more terrorism. Israel immediately refused to release prisoners as well.

After my release, my parents told me how little they knew about hostage negotiations or even if they were occurring at all. Their information was mostly from newspapers, the nightly news, and occasional contact with New York State politicians and the airlines. Their fear, which grew as each day passed, was that they would never see me again.

It's dark again by the time two men in well-worn army fatigues bring dinner, only our second meal of the day, as the food onboard when we left Frankfurt is long gone. The haphazard timing of our meals after only two days on the plane makes me wonder how well our captors have thought through what it takes to house and feed so many hostages, including infants, children, sick people, and those with dietary and religious restrictions. They take several trips up and down the ladder to bring all the food on the plane.

Surprisingly, our meal is noteworthy—a hot dinner courtesy of the Jordanian army—and the smell alone of cooked food is a welcome respite. I gratefully scarf down roast chicken, mashed potatoes, and salad. Bananas

FINAL

DAILY NEWS

NEW YORK'S PICTURE NEWSPAPER

10¢

ARABS HOLD 180 IN HIJACKED JETS

Free 120 Women & Children; Threaten to Blow Up 2 Planes

FIG. 5. Details of the PFLP demands were covered closely in the media. From the PBS American Experience video *Hijacked* (2006).

and grapes are given to the Orthodox Jews who refuse anything else, although there is not sufficient fruit for them all. I wonder if the people who are keeping kosher will soon relent and eat whatever is available. I overhear Irene instructing her sons to save some of the food they are given in case they are not fed again.

After dinner, Bob and I return to speculating about when we'll be released. I'm still upset that I wasn't allowed to go with the other women but, after seeing their releases unfold so quickly, I remain hopeful that our release will be imminent.

Bob does not share my optimism. "I don't know if it's true, but I heard the PFLP laid out demands at the U.S embassy in Amman. They want a prisoner exchange." He lowers his voice. "If their demands aren't met, they're threatening to blow up the planes—with us on board."

I shudder. "Oh Bob, I can't believe they'd do that—it must be a crazy rumor, far outside the realm of the possible." I say this with as much conviction as I can muster. Never mind that the events of the past two days have been equally outside the realm of the possible.

I won't allow myself to think about that. Maybe if I close my eyes, I'll wake up and find this was all a nightmare.

DAY 3

INSPECTION

At midnight, I startle awake when two guerrillas walk down the aisle, a bright flashlight illuminating their way. Bettie, the tall stewardess, follows them. Two rows behind me, they shine the flashlight directly into the face of the man in the aisle seat.

"Jerry Goldman?" Bettie asks.

"Yes, that's me," he whispers.

"Put your shoes on and follow me please," she says apologetically.

With escorts in front and behind, Jerry passes me. His wife, Rebecca, cries as he leaves her and their two-year-old daughter. Jerry is led to the door and ordered to climb down. I wish I could see what was happening outside. Then again, maybe I don't. I remember my own descent from the plane—the adrenaline rush of thinking I was being freed and crashing back to reality when a gun was pointed at me instead.

Over the next half hour, Bettie and the Palestinians identify specific men and remove them from the plane. Bettie looks pained by her actions.

I barely sleep the remainder of the night, on high alert to others who might be taken, listening to the subdued cries of wives and children left behind.

Sadness and fear envelop the plane.

At sunrise, I straighten my increasingly grungy dress and head to the lavatory. Two crew members, Al, our flight engineer, and a stewardess are cleaning the toilets, which have not been flushed for three days. Without water to flush the toilets, the crew is using wooden coat hangers from first class to force down the contents. Now they've run out of hangers, so they're stripping off the wooden panels that cover the walls of the toilet and using the panel pieces to shove the refuse down. Even these extreme measures are hardly working.

Inside the lavatory, I face total darkness. Hovering a few inches above the overflowing bowl, I place one hand on the wall for balance and use the other to hold my nose while I pee quickly. As I head back to my seat, I'm hoping I won't need to go in there again anytime soon.

Bob is standing in the aisle, talking to several men. "Did you hear anything about the guys they took last night?" I ask them.

"Yeah, Al sleeps in first class with the rest of the crew, so he saw the whole thing. Six men were forced off the plane at gunpoint. They blindfolded them, put them in a Land Rover, and drove away. No one knows where they were taken or if they'll return. Four of the men left wives and children on the plane."

"That's awful. Who were they? Why were they singled out?"

"Al talked to their wives. One of the guys is a Jewish chemistry professor from the Bronx. Another works in the U.S. embassy in Algeria and two others work in the Department of Defense in Southeast Asia. Two of them are brothers and rabbis, the Hararis, who teach at a Jewish day school in Flatbush. Their wives, children, and elderly mother are on the plane."

"I think my sister and brother had those rabbis as teachers," I say. "That name sounds familiar." Although I had not spoken with any of the men who'd been taken, hearing details about their lives makes me feel connected to them.

"Why'd they take them in the middle of the night? Did they think we wouldn't notice? Or was it scarier for all of us to do it that way because we don't know who they'll take next?" I ask.

"Don't think that way," Bob says, trying to reassure me. "We're here, we're okay, and we've got no idea what's going to happen. Let's stick with the present."

I've decided by now that I was wrong about Bob. He was the ideal seatmate after all. The voice of reason. I'm thankful he's nearby to ground me when my imagination spins out of control.

About 9:00 a.m. the guerrillas announce we're all getting off the plane to exercise. Younger passengers welcome the opportunity to stretch, but older people ask to stay onboard, especially those with limited mobility. Their requests are denied.

I descend quickly, again hyperaware of my dress. Last time, I heard rumblings from other young women disembarking, warnings of roaming hands and quick feels. Being held hostage is bad enough; the thought of being touched, even momentarily, by any of these men frightens me.

By now, I'm not naive enough to believe this recess is solely for our well-being. Shortly after we're all off the plane, we notice several guerrillas climbing back on. I doubt that they're cleaning up our mess.

On the ground, our captors have literally drawn lines in the sand, which keep us close together, huddled under the narrow wing to block the blazing sun. Cramped again. When two boys playing a game of catch step outside our boundaries, our captors point AK-47s at them. My stomach flips.

"They're just kids having fun!" a mother of one of the boys screams. After that, parents keep their children by their sides.

Though it's our third day being held here, this is the first time any of us have had a chance to really look around, and I'm anxious to glean some hint of civilization from our surroundings.

The desert stretches in every direction, a dark beige with no vegetation, not even small scrub. It's in stark contrast to the green orchards and productive farmland I worked on in Israel. With significant investment from Western countries, Israel had transformed much of its desert into agricultural lands. I wonder if the Palestinians had been farmers and what crops they had grown before they became refugees in surrounding countries.

I strain my ears but can hear no sounds of cars or trucks nearby, no planes overhead. All I see is confirmation that we are far away from everything we know.

Beneath the wing, I play a few listless games of tic-tac-toe with Mike, the college student from Wisconsin with the long wavy hair. We squat and, with our fingers, draw crosses and circles in the sand, keeping a lookout for the guerrillas with guns out of the corners of our eyes. A few Palestinians sprawl on the sand outside the tent. Boredom has set in, even amid so much tension. In the distance, passengers from the Swissair plane also stand under a wing, although there are fewer of them. We have no opportunity to interact.

The guerrillas have painted *PFLP* and *Down with Imperialism* in large letters across the body of our TWA plane. Not on a banner, but on the plane itself. I imagine they did this with brushes and cans of paint while standing on the wings then moving the truck with the ladder along the side of the plane. There is also a line of Arabic writing. I wish I could read what it says, but maybe I'm better off not knowing.

A Palestinian flag, the same as the one in the sand near the tent, has been placed over the American flag on the tail. And draped over the plane's front door is a cloth with the logo of the PFLP. There's an arrow, showing their intent to return to a land they believe is rightfully theirs.

Palestinian sentiments about the right to return are long-standing but intensified as a result of the Six-Day War of 1967, between Israelis and Arabs. During the war, Israel seized significant territories including the Gaza Strip and the West Bank (including East Jerusalem), which meant that all of historic Palestine now came under their control. Israelis became the dominant military power in the region. For the Palestinians, this war resulted in the loss of what remained of their homeland. While I understand this—in the abstract—I don't see what it has to do with us.

Desperate to move despite the heat, I stretch my arms overhead and touch my toes. As sweltering as it's been on the plane, outside is not much better. Without a breeze, the air is stifling in the full sun. For the older people, there's no place to sit except on the hard sand.

Still, like prisoners spending time in the yard, we want to take advantage of the time we have outside. Mike and I wander over to Bob, who is standing with another passenger. Bob introduces us to Ben, a distinguished-looking guy in his midforties with dark hair sprinkled with gray. Ben is traveling with his wife and four children, all under the age of thirteen, and his father-in-law.

"How's the exercise going?" Bob asks.

"I'm exhausted from my workout," I half joke. My lips are parched, and I'm badly in need of water. I'm also hungry but there's no point in bringing that up. I'm pretty sure everyone else is feeling the same. I lower my voice. "What do you think the commandos are doing on the plane?"

"People think they're going through our hand luggage," Ben says, "but I'm betting Bassam and his buddies are watching the movie we were supposed to see on our flight to New York. Yup, they're relaxing, enjoying those soft seats in first class."

"Sounds about right," I say. I can tell that Ben is a guy whose sense of humor I'll enjoy.

When we reboard, the plane is messier than it was before, with our belongings strewn haphazardly on the seats and floor. Bags have been pulled from the overhead compartments, and items that were under our seats have been opened, the contents removed.

We rummage through our bags to see what's missing. My earlier fears are immediately realized: My Israeli army shirt is gone. There's no sign of my address book and journal, either. My small Kodak camera has been opened, exposing the film. A photography book of the ancient site of Masada, a place of Jewish resistance, is gone. So is the skullcap with gold-threaded embroidery I purchased as a souvenir gift for my brother, Joel. I put what remains back in the bag and stash it in the overhead compartment, trying not to worry what it means that all my lost belongings are items with direct ties to Israel.

But all around me, my fellow passengers are exclaiming over their own missing items, buzzing with the same conclusions.

It does not take long before our captors confirm our suspicions.

Standing in the front of the plane, Bassam announces with his bullhorn that they have found many items in passengers' bags that show connections to the Israeli army and Zionism. As proof, he holds up a Six-Day War pin and a medal with Israeli General Moshe Dayan's face etched on it. Nobody moves to reclaim these items—of course not. Why would they? Our faces burn as Bassam demands that any remaining items from Israel in our bags should be turned over immediately. They plan to conduct another search; now is the time to come forward.

The guerrillas who carried out the inspection leave us, and chaos erupts.

Their search has not been especially thorough. But we all fear the next one will be.

My attention is drawn to a distraught college student named David. He is traveling with his mother and three younger siblings, and he looks terrified as he extracts the Israeli army uniform they have overlooked in his carry-on bag.

David beckons one of the crew members. I'm sitting close by and watch as he shows Al, the flight engineer, the uniform. "What can I do with this? I'm in big trouble if they find it in a later search." It's clear that any other personal belongings suggesting ties to the military will not be viewed favorably by the commandos.

Al gently places his hand on David's shoulder to calm him. "I'll get rid of it for you. Don't worry." I wondered how he'd do it. Maybe the crew have secret places on board where Al knows the uniform won't be discovered.

But if it is, what will the reprisals be? Do our lives depend on what we do—or don't do—in this moment? I knew enough to worry about my army shirt earlier, but I hadn't thought of giving it to a crew member; Al might have taken mine too. I'd observed that the commandos treated the crew differently—more friendly than they were to the passengers. I doubt that any of their bags were inspected. I wonder if the crew are secretly as afraid of the PFLP as the rest of us are.

A rabbi with a long white beard and a black hat stands on his seat, carefully searching the overhead compartment. A younger man, his son-in-law, is helping him search for the manuscript of his latest book, which is missing.

When they can't find it anywhere, the rabbi approaches Bassam, who has just returned to the plane. The rabbi insists, begs, that the PFLP return the manuscript to him.

"That's my life's work," the distraught rabbi says in accented English. "It's of no use to you, and it's in Yiddish. What could you possibly want with pages written in a language you don't understand?"

Bassam dismisses his request. "We may return it to you later, but now, go back to your seat."

The grief-stricken rabbi complies.

I have empathy for him; last school year, one of my college girlfriends managed to lose a typed forty-page thesis she had yet to turn in. She had notes on the topic but struggled to recreate what she had written. I can't even imagine how this rabbi will face rewriting a whole book.

But perhaps it's a moot point. Perhaps the bigger worry is whether he'll ever make it home to his typewriter at all.

In the early afternoon, a man in a pressed beige linen suit arrives, introducing himself as Andre Rochat, a representative of the International Committee of the Red Cross (ICRC), the parent organization of the Red Crescent. Mr. Rochat, a well-built Swiss national, speaks Arabic with the Palestinians and gives us the good news that negotiations for our release are proceeding.

I didn't know it then, but Andre Rochat was the chief executive of the ICRC, tasked with overseeing an area extending from Morocco to Afghanistan. Initially, the Swiss and West German governments had agreed to free imprisoned Palestinians held in their countries, but after consultation with the U.S. and British governments, they withdrew from the agreement. The four nations decided the ICRC would handle negotiations with the PFLP. Rochat's role was to negotiate for the release of all hostages regardless of nationality—meaning that Israeli passengers must have the same status as the rest. It was one more example of how we all became pawns in a delicate international situation that none of us could fully grasp.

With Mr. Rochat onboard, postcards and pens are distributed, and we're instructed to write short messages to our families. I sit for a minute thinking what I should write. Maybe it doesn't matter; I'm skeptical the postcard will ever reach my parents. But everyone around me is taking the opportunity seriously, so I allay my cynicism. With false cheer, I write:

> Dear Mom and Dad,
>
> I want you to know that I'm okay. We're still on the plane in the Jordanian desert. I hope you know that they already sent some women and children home and I hope I'll be in the next group to leave. Please don't worry too much. I'm thinking of you, miss you, and will be so happy when I'm finally home!
>
> Love and kisses, Mimi

A few passengers volunteer to help hand out box lunches, courtesy of the ICRC. It's the first food we've had all day and a welcome distraction. The cheese and jam sandwich on pita bread, handful of grapes, and small bottle of water calm my frayed nerves and growling stomach.

After lunch, an English-speaking Palestinian doctor is allowed onto the plane, and he makes rounds inquiring about our health. Though he is kind and caring about our well-being, his questions are absurd. How does he think we are, as captives on a 120-degree plane for three days with limited food and water, filthy toilets, horrible smells, and worry for our lives? I've heard people say they're feeling dizzy or have headaches, which could signal dehydration or heat stroke. Some elderly people are complaining that they need a regular supply of water to take their pills. We're all thirsty. Even kids understand how precious water is here. When a young boy spilled his allotted cup, he cried, worried whether he could get more.

Waiting for our release is difficult enough for a twenty-year-old like me; what about mothers with crying babies and toddlers who can't sit in a seat for two minutes, let alone three days? Or women who have seen their husbands removed at gunpoint, not knowing whether they'll see them again? Or the two young sisters traveling alone who have dust and allergy problems and desperately need their medicine? And the Orthodox Jews who are hardly eating and growing weaker by the day? While physical health is low on my list of immediate concerns, I understand that others' circumstances are more serious.

Fortunately, the doctor hands out aspirin and tranquilizers to anyone who wants them. In college, my roommate, Karen, always had a bottle of Valium on hand, and I sometimes took one to relax and space out. I liked how it lightened my spirits when I was uptight about exams or classwork. I take several pills from the doctor, anticipating a future need. He promises to bring diapers and alcohol to clean the babies as well as insulin for people with diabetes. There is also mention of immunizing all of us against cholera, as there is an epidemic raging in the region.

I'm not planning on getting any vaccinations here but, then again, maybe it would be scarier not to. I know I got some extra vaccinations before venturing abroad, though I was told they took a couple of weeks to start to work.

"Hey Bob, what do you know about cholera?" I ask.

Bob looks serious. "You can get cholera from poor sanitation and contaminated drinking water. You get diarrhea and you're dehydrated."

"Well, that sounds exactly like our situation. Some people already have diarrhea. And what's this about immunizing us? Since when does an immunization work so quickly?" I ask.

"It doesn't, not to my knowledge anyway. But let's not get ahead of ourselves." Bob gives me his calm half smile, like he's trying to convince himself, too.

In the late afternoon, there's a miraculous event. A truck with a generator arrives and, with some difficulty, it's hooked up to the plane. Emergency doors are closed so the air conditioner can be turned on. As the cool air begins to circulate, we cheer and clap. I feel more energized than I have in days. All around the plane, people are smiling, relieved not to be sweating. Lethargy is lifting. Maybe the doctor has informed his PFLP comrades that it's dangerous for us to bake in the sweltering heat of the plane for hours and days on end.

However this miracle happened, we are thrilled and hopeful that this new level of cool comfort will continue. It's one less thing to worry about.

While the generator is working, crew members flush the toilets for the first time since we've landed. It's clear that if we continue to stay onboard, there will need to be a better solution to this sanitation problem. As relieved as we are to have ventilation back on the plane, the air conditioning brings the putrid smell of the toilets into the cabin, particularly for those seated in the rear of the plane. I shudder to think of the related health hazard. Fortunately, I'm not the only one. Al asks Bassam to get his men to dig a trench in the sand under the toilets. After they complete the task, the crew empties the toilets out fully, dropping the fetid contents into the sand. The stench is reduced—another act of mercy.

Unfortunately, after an hour or so, the generator stops working, and it's not long before we are once again broiling in our oven. Our reversal in fortune has been temporary, and the mood in the cabin quickly turns back to disappointment and despair.

Well, not for everyone. Those who've taken tranquilizers seem to be okay. I haven't taken one yet; I'm saving for future panics.

Over the next few days, the generator is turned on now and then for short periods of fifteen minutes to an hour. Part of the problem is that to run the generator, our pilot needs to use jet fuel, which he wants to conserve in case we're allowed to take off. The Swissair pilot has kindly agreed to let the generator be used only for our plane as we have more passengers, including many women and children.

But I refuse to let these circumstances get the best of me again. I speak with Rachel and we agree it's time for action to lift our spirits. We round up some of the kids—eight of them—and find a space in the back where we can gather. Shoshana, a college student from Yeshiva University, joins as a "camp" counselor. She's a great addition to our team; she has experience working with children of all ages and knows how to teach them to sing in harmony. With Shoshana's guidance, we sing "Row, Row, Row Your Boat" in rounds with the older kids and "London Bridge" with the younger ones. Shoshana changes the lyrics of John Denver's popular song "*Leaving* on a Jet Plane" to reflect our situation: "*Living* on a Jet Plane." Suddenly it sounds as if we're almost joyful that we don't know when we'll be back again.

Our fun abruptly ends when we are ordered to return to our seats. Our captors' moods have darkened. As it turns out, eliminating the waste from the plane has not been such a blessing after all—amid the mess, they have spotted bits of Israeli passports and Hebrew documents. This renews their suspicions about who is onboard—and what else we are keeping from them.

From what I've heard and seen in recent days, there is some reason for their heightened suspicions. The men who work for the U.S. Department of Defense tore up sensitive documents and dropped them in the toilet before they were taken off the plane. One of the young girls traveling alone has dual citizenship. Too young to understand the potential harm, her seatmate, a savvy college student, acted on her behalf by ripping up her Israeli passport, swallowing the identification pages, and shoving tiny pieces into the shit-filled toilet. Just like the people across the aisle from me had done. Who knows? Probably other passengers did the same. Whatever it took to save their lives.

But now, the commandos are furious, desperate to find out who these people are who ripped up their passports. I turn to Bob. "There's only so much you can hide on a plane," I say. "Things are gonna get worse." I'm hoping Bob will be able to squash my negative thoughts, the way he's done in the past.

But he doesn't. Not this time.

After a silence, he replies, "You're right. The PFLP's whole strategy for the hijacking was to find those dual citizens and Israelis and use them as bargaining chips in their negotiations with Israel and other countries, so their comrades can be freed. They're gonna do whatever it takes to find out who those people are."

A wave of panic washes over me. Bob's words ring true. But how will the guerrillas identify these people? And then, what will they do with them?

I suddenly remember the upbeat message I wrote on the postcard to my parents, saying everything was okay. What a joke. Nothing was okay. But I'd been socialized to say that. I'd learned how to shove my real feelings down, to keep them hidden.

DAY 4

INTERROGATION

At night, the plane is dimly lit by one kerosene lamp, which hangs in the middle of the aisle. With the cabin darkened, tears flood my cheeks. I hope no one can see them. We're all in the same situation, and I don't want to call attention to myself. Anyway, I'm not the type, if there is one, who cries in public. I mostly show a happy face to the world—the Mimi who is friendly, chatty, who likes to laugh about things.

Right now, what I really want, really need, is a hot shower, a toothbrush and toothpaste, clean underwear, a T-shirt, and my purple bell-bottoms. Then maybe I'd feel better.

Sleep, when it comes, is interrupted by the snoring and phlegm-filled coughing around me. Some men stretch out on the floor beneath their seats, their legs reaching into the aisle. A few lie down right in the aisle, using their jackets for pillows. Women remain in their seats. I'm tempted to join the men on the floor but can't do it with a short dress on. That damn green minidress—of all the things! It echoes like a mean, tiresome joke.

The crew and a few guerrillas spend each night in the first-class cabin, curtains drawn. The passengers in the front of the economy section say they hear talking late into the night and suspect the guerrillas and crew are drinking alcohol or consuming what food remains in the first-class galley.

In the morning, I visit my friend Mike, who is sitting by himself in an emergency exit row. The seating is fluid on the airplane now, so I'm comfortable changing my seat whenever I feel like it. Mike is traveling alone, like me. He makes me laugh; I crave moments when fear can be pushed to the margins. Many young women on the plane are religious and traveling with their families. In my experience, Orthodox Jewish girls and women can be condescending toward less observant women who appear immodest. Even as a young girl in the yeshiva, I remember how some girls gave me dirty looks when my knees and elbows showed.

Midmorning, when our aluminum shell heats up, Mike and I remove the emergency exit door as the crew did and stash the heavy door in a nearby empty row. The occasional breeze is welcome, but when the wind picks up, sand blows into the plane. In the time it takes to put the door back in place, sand enters our eyes and ears, a fine layer settling on our already dirty and dusty clothes. The crunch of fine sand lingers in my mouth.

Our captors bring plastic bags containing a familiar small breakfast: half a pita bread and a hard-boiled egg for each of us. Mike makes light of the food. "If only they'd give us raw eggs," he says, "I'd jump out on the wing and cook up some omelets on our very own griddle!"

I giggle, playing along. "While you're out there making the omelet, would you mind heating up my tea? These lukewarm beverages are not up to my standards."

"Sure, and perhaps you'd prefer a crumpet instead of pita bread? I'll bring it to you in a minute, madam!"

Our living conditions improve when the Red Cross delivers the provisions flown in the previous day. Among the urgently needed supplies are diapers, rubbing alcohol, bottle sterilizers, formula and jars of baby food for the increasingly hungry, dirty, smelly babies, and toilet paper and cologne to spray in the lavatories. We are glad to see cases of bottled water, orange and lemon soda, canned meats, jam, fruits, powdered milk, bread, and watermelons. Stress relievers are also included: aspirin, tranquilizers, and cigarettes.

The passenger work crew prepares and distributes plates of bread, jam, lunch meat, and watermelon slices for lunch, along with warm soda or water. For the Orthodox Jews, they prepare plates of bread, jam, and fruit. The religious couple across the aisle, who have been eating only bread, readily accept watermelon.

As I take my last bite of a jam sandwich, a young female guerrilla stops at my seat. Clutching a gun in her hand, she asks, "Mimi Beeber?"

I dig my nails into the armrests. "Yes, that's me."

Mike puts his hand over mine and squeezes it.

"Come with me, right now."

I stand, my legs shaking, my heart thumping. I am in the aisle seat, and as I slowly get up, I keep my eyes firmly fixed on her gun.

Maybe she is taking me off the plane, like they did to all those men during the night.

Gesturing for me to walk in front of her, she stays close behind, pressing her gun hard into my lower back. It feels cold through my cotton dress.

She pulls aside the curtain to the first-class cabin and pushes me into a seat.

An older man, a gun in hand, moves close to me. I have not seen this short, gray-haired man before. He has a scraggly beard and a thick, jagged scar running across his cheek. A kaffiyeh is wrapped around his head, wisps of coarse hair poking out around his ears.

"Mimi Beeber, we know you are a member of the Israeli army."

My hands are trembling, and I tuck them under my thighs, hoping he won't notice.

"No, no. I'm an American. I'm from New York. I'm a college student." Better to keep my responses short than incriminate myself by providing too much information.

He stares at my face, his expression stern. His voice drips with contempt. "You're lying. We found your Israeli army shirt. The backpack you have is from the Israeli army, the kind given to soldiers."

I try not to show any emotion, not to give away the panic that has grabbed hold of my entire body, making my shaking worse.

He moves his gun to rest on my temple. "Tell the truth now or this will be the end of you."

I swallow hard and squeeze my eyes shut for a second to stop myself from bursting into tears.

"No, no, I swear, that shirt isn't mine. It was in my bag, yes, but it's not mine. My friend who was in the army gave it to me. I'm not Israeli and I'm not in their army." My voice quivers so much it sounds foreign to me.

Before the hijacking, the only time I'd seen a gun was on television and now there was one resting on my forehead. Is he just trying to frighten me, so I'll reveal who he thinks I *really am*? My only consolation is that they haven't shot anyone yet. Perhaps foolishly, I doubt I'll be the first.

Sweat is dripping from my armpits, settling near my waist. I take a deep breath, determined to try again to prove my innocence to this man. "And the backpack—I got it in the market in Tel Aviv the day before I left. I just needed a bag to bring gifts home for my family. I'm American. You have my passport. Look at it, you'll see I was born in the United States."

He brings his mouth close to my ear and shouts, "Do you think we're stupid? We have pictures of you in your uniform with your army comrades. How can you deny this?" He's so angry, veins are bulging from his neck.

Till that moment, I'd totally forgotten that I had stashed some photos of myself with kibbutz friends in the pocket of my journal; only now I remember that in one picture, I wore an army shirt. I'd put it on to look like my Israeli friends wearing their uniforms. They had just completed their two-year military service, happy to be done but proud they had served.

I know it looks bad. But he's wrong about me. I scramble, trying to think of some other proof in my bag that this isn't what it seems. But I've spent the entire summer in Israel. Of course I have mementos of that time in my bag.

The interrogator removes his gun from my forehead. I hope it's a signal that the interrogation is over.

Unexpectedly, he switches to Hebrew. "*Ei-foh ha-darkon hayisraeli?*"

I understand the question—*Where's the Israeli passport?*—but stare ahead. It feels like a test, that I'll automatically respond in Hebrew, as an Israeli or a dual citizen might. I flash on the Orthodox couple who cut up their passports. Maybe he believes I did the same.

I stare directly back. Eye contact has never felt more uncomfortable, but maybe I'll appear more truthful if I look him squarely in the face. "I don't understand what you're saying. I speak English, not Hebrew. If you want to ask me questions, ask in English. It's the only language I speak."

"You're a Zionist?" he asks.

For religious Jews like my parents, Israel is the "promised land," and they are in complete support of a Jewish state in the Middle East. I want to believe that people can coexist peacefully even if history tells us differently. In this moment, all I know is that I must deny every accusation he flings at me. My life depends on it.

"I'm not a Zionist, I'm a student. I went to Israel to travel, to see the country, that's it. Just a tourist trip to see the sights. I worked on a farm, a kibbutz. I don't know anything about Zionism. I'm not Israeli, I'm not in their army. What can I say to convince you?" After a moment, I add, "I believe in peace, not war."

"You're a liar! Why should we believe you?" he shouts, his sour spit wetting my cheek. "We found your address book—full of names of Israelis, your friends, your family, your people."

"Sure, I met people when I traveled around the country. That is who is in the picture with me. And when I left the kibbutz, people gave me their addresses and phone numbers. But that doesn't make me a Zionist or an Israeli soldier. I swear it."

Is he trying to wear me down with a barrage of questions to catch me in an inconsistency? How can I defend myself against a conclusion he has already reached?

The interrogator's dark eyes narrow. "We're watching you and we will continue this conversation. We're not finished here."

The woman who brought me up to the front earlier nudges me in the arm. I stand and follow her.

I just make it back to the seat next to Mike before my legs buckle.

"I was so worried. You've been gone an awful long time," Mike says. "You're white as a ghost."

I take some deep breaths, fighting a waterfall of tears that want to flow.

"They found that army shirt my friend gave me and my army issue backpack and accused me of being an Israeli soldier! They found pictures I'd forgotten about with army friends and my address book. The guy—Scarface—had a gun to my head . . ."

Mike reaches for my hand. "All the stuff they found when they searched the plane and emptied the toilets really set them off. Look, they're bringing Mrs. Raab for questioning now. I think they're going to be interrogating a lot of us. But we'll get through it, I promise."

I swallow a tranquilizer I stashed in my dress pocket and close my eyes. The interrogator's seething anger still pulses through my body. I am no longer a tourist returning from a summer's journey; I am their enemy. If only I could explain who I am, they'd see they've pegged me wrong. Before I went to Israel, I spent weekends protesting with the Vietnam Veterans Against the War in DC. I was against U.S. imperialism in Southeast Asia. Just one year ago, I marched with over a quarter of a million others in the Moratorium to End the War in Vietnam in DC. Our multicultural group walked down Pennsylvania Avenue, passing by the White House. We were led by Coretta Scott King in this peaceful march, where we carried candles to express our grief and sadness about the war. The names of the dead were read out loud so we would remember the magnitude of the loss.

The idea I'd join any army, no matter where it was, is so far from the truth, it's almost insulting. It chips away at my identity, making me feel truly lost.

Throughout the day, other passengers are brought to the first-class section for interrogation. When they come back, they, too, are drained of color and trembling as they share with the rest of us what happened. Mrs. Raab, who is traveling with her four children, faces unrelenting questions about Hadassah membership cards in her wallet. Finding she was a member over a three-year period, the guerrillas conclude she holds an important role in the organization. They demand to know what the group is and what position she has. She tries to explain that Hadassah is a Jewish women's group that raises money for hospitals to help Jews and Arabs in Israel, serving all who need their assistance. They don't believe her, just as they didn't believe me. She, too, vehemently denies being a Zionist, fearful that the PFLP will not hesitate to kill her or any other passenger onboard.

Ben is also interrogated. I learn the details from Bob, who has become his fast friend. In his hand luggage, the Palestinians found an Israeli bond in his son's name that he brought to Israel to cash. Ben had forgotten all about it; he has no defense at the ready. They accuse him of being an American imperialist helping to fund the Israeli army. The interrogator demands that Ben tell everything about the family trip to Israel, insisting he reveal names and addresses of all the people and places they visited during their stay. He suspects Ben has a relative who is a general in the Israeli army. Like many of us, he is warned that they are not done questioning him.

Frightened as I am, I try to keep the perspective that, so far, they have not acted on their threats. I don't want to acknowledge the possibility that they could actually pull the trigger on that gun they are holding to our heads. I hardly know the other passengers on the plane, but I am certain those who are older understand more about our situation than I do. Some have experienced violence, discrimination in finding employment, and other forms of antisemitism. Irene is not the only concentration camp survivor in our company, and others quietly identify themselves as children of Holocaust survivors.

Growing up in a mostly Jewish enclave in Brooklyn in the 1950s and '60s, I was shielded from the experiences of the generations before me. Although my grandparents, my father, and other family members had escaped persecution in Russia and Romania in the early twentieth century, they did not talk about their experiences. They, like others in the neighborhood, sent their children to religious schools and Jewish summer camps, where a cultural identity was fostered. I was not burdened by the collective traumatic memory shared by Jews across the world, memories lodged in their identity.

Now, I'm surrounded by them. They know all too well what can happen, but no one wants to talk about it. Their stories remain in the shadows, quietly humbling us. We need to stay strong for each other.

The interrogations are mostly of Jewish passengers, but non-Jews are also questioned. Bob has never spent time in Israel but is accused of being a staunch supporter of the country, and the Palestinians demand to know why he continues to travel there. His rationale that his passport represents nothing more than his stamp-collecting hobby is dismissed by the interrogator as a poor excuse.

In the afternoon, we learn our pilot and copilot, James Woods and Jim Majer, have been ordered to assist in landing a third plane at Revolution Airport. A BOAC VC10 flying from Bombay to London has been hijacked on the Bahrain-to-Beirut leg of its flight. We spot the plane as it makes its descent and circles the runway, seeking a safe place to land. With some difficulty, the TWA pilots guide the BOAC plane to land safely. As the dust settles on the airstrip, PFLP vehicles speed toward the plane. A large crowd of guerrillas gather with their guns held high, embracing one another in celebration of their latest accomplishment. We are astonished and bereft that they have managed yet another hijacking. Are we not collateral enough? Why have they taken another plane when our own situation is so quickly deteriorating?

This does indeed prove to be the bad sign we fear: We don't know it yet, but the PFLP's initial demands for the release of Palestinian prisoners have not been met. They have hardened their position, not only taking more hostages but adding to their demands the release of hundreds of political prisoners held in Israel. They are threatening more hijackings, warning the world there is "additional space for more hijacked planes at Revolution Airport." The BOAC jet is the first indication of them making good on that threat.

That evening, Hannah hears on the radio that President Nixon is giving Phantom jets—fighter aircraft using radar and missile technology—to

Israel. She still is keeping her radio well hidden, listening only when the Palestinians are not around and keeping the rest of us posted through a risky game of telephone. Evidently, the Israelis requested the jets a year ago, but Nixon has strategically chosen this moment to provide them, presumably to send a message to the PFLP that the United States stands with Israel. Furious at this development because it provides enhanced technology for the Israelis, our captors scream at us, once again, to return to our seats. Bassam announces that the PFLP is no longer responsible for our safety, a portent of terrors yet to come.

The mood on the plane is one of confusion as well as fear. Because we are unaware of the specifics of the PFLP's demands in exchange for the passengers and other developments, their behavior seems terrifyingly arbitrary, calm one minute, in a fury the next. Only in hindsight would we fully grasp the terrifying dance of cause and effect going on behind the scenes. Again and again, the PFLP kept extending their deadlines for their comrades' release. Again and again, various governments would refuse to comply, and their anger would flare and intensify.

DAY 5

UNCERTAINTY

In the early morning I slowly wake, holding on to a dream. I am standing on a rocky precipice high above a calm blue sea, seagulls flying gracefully overhead. There are other people there, too, mostly young, laughing and smiling, eager for their turn to plunge into the water. Curling my toes around the warm granite rock, I pause at the edge before I jump. I yell with the joy of abandon as I fall toward the sea. My feet hit the warm water and my body submerges. I pop up smiling, ready to do it again.

I open my eyes, and for one moment everything feels better.

Then it fades.

I head toward the back of the plane, hoping the ache in my lower stomach is from hunger—we had no dinner last night—but fear I'm getting my period. It's been five days since I left Tel Aviv, and I assumed I'd be home by now. I have tampons in my checked bag but don't know how to retrieve them.

How will I figure out if I have my period in the pitch-dark bathroom? Eventually a red stain on my green dress will appear, but by then it will be too late to avoid embarrassment. I cling to the modicum of self-respect I still have, which is not much considering I haven't brushed my teeth, washed my face and hands, or changed my clothes in five days.

Passing by Rachel's seat, I whisper, "Have you got a tampon? I may have gotten my period."

Rachel looks at me, her eyes warm with compassion. "You poor thing. I don't use tampons, but I've got a sanitary napkin I can give you."

"Thanks. Great timing, huh? Can I sit next to you while you're looking? I don't want to call attention to myself by standing in the aisle."

Rachel bends over to open her backpack, and her hair falls into her face. I notice an Arabic book inside.

"You read Arabic?" I ask, surprised.

"Yeah, I was born in Khartoum—in the Sudan where my family lived for many years."

"Oh, wow."

I know Sudan is in Africa but am unsure where exactly. Despite my interest in being a world traveler, my knowledge of geography is limited. I make a mental note to become more proficient when I get home. If I get home.

"Why'd your family leave?" I ask.

"Sudan got its independence from Britain in the 1950s. When the British left, there was a lot of antisemitism, so most Jews left for the U.S., Europe, or Israel. My family came to the U.S. when I was young. I understand Arabic and can speak it well."

"Can you understand the guerrillas when they're talking to each other?"

"Mostly, but their dialect is different. They speak a Palestinian Arabic, and what I speak is closer to an Egyptian Arabic. But I understand almost all of what they say."

"Good to know," I reply, not sure if it is an advantage or not. I'm a little afraid to ask if she's overheard anything truly alarming. "What's that book about?"

"I've been taking a course at college for the past two semesters. Rutgers has an Arabic language program, so I'm improving my reading and writing skills. It was challenging at first, but it's getting easier now."

She pulls out a half-empty blue package of Stayfree beltless sanitary napkins.

"Just take one for now in case I need them later," Rachel says. "You don't need a belt—they just stick to your panties. I have a little flashlight—do you want to take it with you?"

"Thank you so much, I don't know what I'd do without you!" I stash the pad and light in my pocket, hoping the bulge will escape the guard's notice. Yesterday, a guard didn't let Susie into the toilet with her purse. He was suspicious, but she was only trying to be subtle about her own sanitary napkin. It's yet another indignity the men on board don't need to worry about.

Never mind that I've never even used a pad before. When I got my period at fourteen, my older sister gave me a thirty-second demonstration of how to insert a tampon, shoved me into the bathroom, stationed herself outside the door, and instructed me not to come out till it was in. I favor trendy, tight clothes and never imagined wearing a pad that might create a visible bulge. But I guess the Orthodox women on board don't share that concern. Their loose-fitting clothing is intended to mask their body shapes, lest they distract men from their religious studies. And in my yeshiva class in sixth and seventh grades, an age when all my classmates were first getting their periods, I remember them whispering about tampons being taboo, tampering with a girl's all-important virginity.

The first time I got my period, I went into my parents' bedroom to tell my mother.

"I finally got my period!" I said excitedly. Most of my girlfriends already had theirs, and I was getting worried.

She slapped me hard across the face. It stung and I started crying.

"Mazel Tov!" she said, smiling.

"Why'd you hit me?" I asked. It was something she never did.

"It's Jewish custom. It's supposed to wake up a girl who's just gotten her period to the importance of being careful around boys."

"I don't get it," I said, hoping for more.

She didn't respond. Our bodies were just another topic we'd never talk about, not then, not ever.

I head to the back of the plane where, fortunately, there are no guards. I enter the toilet and balance the borrowed flashlight on the edge of the waterless sink to verify that my menstrual cycle has indeed chosen this poor timing. Even as I attach the pad to my panties, I know it's a temporary solution. With no idea how long it will suffice, I head to the galley to ask Mary if they have tampons on board.

"Mary, I have a problem."

"Yeah, you and everybody else on this plane," she mutters. I must have grimaced because she catches herself and asks, "How can I help?" with a well-rehearsed smile that would have made TWA proud.

"I got my period, and the only tampons I have with me are in my luggage. Have you got any?"

"I'll see what I can round up for you. What seat are you in?"

"For now, I'm in row 10. Thanks!" I return to the row where Mike is eating breakfast.

As I settle into my seat, I notice that Mike's hair is a mess and he's badly in need of a shave. It's probably how I look, too, like I've been living under a bridge for a couple of weeks. Not only is my dress filthy, but I must have caught it on something last time I climbed down the ladder. It's developed a decent-size rip next to the front pocket.

"Good morning," Mike says, smiling. "They gave out food while you were gone. I took a bag for you and filled your cup with water. I've got to warn you that the water tastes like it came from a swimming pool. It's so chlorinated—I had to spit it out. Beware."

I wince at the warning. My thirst is reaching a new high. Still, I thank him for looking out for me. The delicacies of the morning include our usual: pita bread filled with crumbled feta cheese and a spoonful of sweet strawberry jam, a hard-boiled egg, and a small clump of wrinkled red grapes. Mike keeps up an amusing running commentary. Today he focuses on the grapes, "elderly and in no condition to be on board."

I close my eyes and fantasize about blackout chocolate cake from Ebinger's bakery, where I'd go with my mother on Friday afternoons. That gooey, rich chocolate layer cake, iced with fudge and sprinkled with cake crumbs, was my go-to Saturday morning breakfast, followed with a cold milk chaser. My mother had told me that Mr. Ebinger, who had grown up in Germany, named the cake "blackout" because his family had lived for long periods without electricity during World War II.

Like us now.

Bassam announces that they are going to call people off the plane in groups to search our checked luggage. Elderly people are permitted to stay on board if family members can identify their suitcases. I'm ready to be outside, away from the aluminum oven I've been baking in for 120 hours.

It's becoming more of a feat to get off the plane each time we descend. The old wooden ladder is unsteady, and some of the rungs are sagging under the weight of passengers and guerrillas going up and down for the past five days. More than one passenger has slipped, requiring attention for cuts and sprains from a Palestinian doctor.

Our suitcases are lined up in the sand. Ramy and two other guerrillas in green fatigues and kaffiyehs are tasked with luggage inspection. My well-used orange Kelty backpack with its external metal frame is easy to spot amid hundreds of blue, green, and gray hard-shell suitcases. Ramy unties my pack, opens the flap, and dumps the contents on the sand. I want to smack him for treating my things so carelessly—but remain a silent witness.

He throws my belongings into piles: items of Israeli origin in one, personal items like clothes and toiletries in another. There is a special

FIG. 6. Passengers from the British Overseas Airways Corporation (BOAC) plane prepare to descend the ladder by holding on to the rope. The Palestinian flag and the PFLP logo are near the door. *Newsweek*, September 21, 1970.

box for passengers' gold watches, chains, bracelets, and silver jewelry. Maybe they'll be sold to support their movement, or divided up among the guerrillas? I imagine them melting them down like the Nazis did with looted Jewish gold.

First to go into the Israel pile are maps and tourist brochures I planned to use to make a memory collage of my summer. Next come rolls of exposed film. Letters for my parents from relatives in Israel and a gift from my Uncle Benzion and Aunt Mitzi. I stand helpless as they confiscate dangling filagree earrings I chose for my college roommate, an ornately embroidered white blouse for Debi, a prayer shawl with special twined and knotted fringes for my father, and a multicolored menorah for my mother. I worked hard to select these things for people I love, but he treats them as inconsequential, unworthy of giving as gifts to others.

Ramy's eyebrows lower and pinch together as he stares at the contents of a small white box that contains a bronze medallion commemorating the Six-Day War, with the two commanders in charge etched on the coin. The corners of his lips narrow.

"Moshe Dayan and Yitzhak Rabin," he sneers, recognizing them. "Enemies of the Palestinian people!" He tosses the medallion forcefully into the Israeli pile, as if I'm an enemy, too.

The medallion is a gift from my soldier friend Ari, the one who also gave me the army shirt. I doubt I'd wear the medallion at home, but it's a memory of our friendship. I know these are only "things," but they have meaning for me. Observing Ramy's anger, I understand that this small memento has meaning for him as well; it signifies more than I realized, the defeat of the combined armies of Jordan, Syria, and Egypt by Israel. The loss of more land to Israel.

At the bottom of my pack, he finds the tampon box. He removes a few from their wrappers and gives me a quizzical look. I crudely point to my vagina with an upward motion, demonstrating how a tampon is used. Ramy's face reddens in embarrassment, and he throws the remaining tampons in the toiletry pile. Reaching over to grab them does not seem like an option; he's got a gun. I wince at his disregard for a harmless product I need, but tampons are not worth angering him. I can only hope Mary can retrieve them later. She brought me a few tampons earlier and I stashed them in my seat pocket, but I know they won't be enough if we're here much longer.

When he's done looking through my bag, he shoves the non-Israeli items, now sprinkled with sand, back into my backpack.

Mrs. Raab and her family are next in line. Ramy finds a bag of Israeli caramels in one of their suitcases, starts eating one, and offers them to his comrades. Suddenly, he spits out the half-chewed candy.

"Ptui, Ptui!" Turning my head, I catch a glimpse of Ramy's half-chewed candy heading toward Mrs. Raab's foot. It lands an inch from her big toe.

"I spit on Israel, I spit on Zionism, I spit on Jews," Ramy says. His comrades follow suit.

Cringing, Mrs. Raab steps back from the gooey mess. I look away, embarrassed for her. For all of us.

Standing under the blazing sun, sweating, and dehydrated from days of limited drinking water, we are weak and faint. Captain Woods insists that our captors place chairs next to their "inspection center" so we don't collapse. Copilot Jim distributes shapely green bottles of Coca-Cola. I'm not sure how they've suddenly appeared, but I welcome the familiar taste of home, even if it is too warm for my liking. The sugar rush buoys my spirits.

I wait, trying not to show the impatience boiling inside me, as the suitcase search continues. I'm becoming more desperate by the minute to head to the restroom, worrying that blood might soon come trickling, or, worse yet, flowing, down my leg.

Captain Woods instructs the crew to release the life rafts onto the desert floor. As if by magic, two bright yellow rubber boats appear, inflating as they drop from the plane. Some of the children jump inside them, bouncing around as if these are trampolines. The crew put up the raft's shade cloth to block the direct sun.

Three girls take the strap that was tied around the raft and use it as a jump rope. They each take a turn, laughing. To our amazement, one of the young male Palestinians who's been standing nearby breaks in to have a turn. He's good at it; maybe he plays this with his sisters. For a few moments we're grinning, like we're on the same playing field, enjoying a game together.

"Mimi, Rachel, Shoshana, come play with us," a girl shouts. I hesitate for a few seconds and then jump on the trampoline. I grab the hand of one of the girls, which helps me stay upright. Then, I jump out, remembering my "problem."

"*Whee, whee, yahoo!*" yell the bouncing kids.

Hearing their giggles, shrieks, and gales of laughter brings smiles to our faces.

When we reboard, Bassam instructs two guards to hook up the plane to the generator. After the hours spent outside in the heat of the day, we need to get cool.

My stomach growls loudly. The passengers in charge of meals distribute what they can, not knowing how much they need to reserve. We each receive half a pita bread with a dollop of jam and a cup of warm orange soda.

An eleven-year-old girl is growing feverish, and the crew requests that the Palestinian doctor come on board to examine her. Her mother sits by her side as the doctor gives her an injection and a bottle of water, a scarce resource. Soon, she dozes off. Maybe he gave her part of a tranquilizer, too. There's a rumor going around that providing them to people on the plane is a strategy for keeping us calm. It sure helped me when I needed one.

"I appreciate your coming to help my daughter," the mother says, teary eyed.

The doctor nods in response and turns to his next patients: an elderly woman who feels faint, a teenage boy who has asthma and has exhausted his medication, and several passengers who have diarrhea. Those who are treated thank the doctor for his kind treatment and dispensing of medicines.

It is surprising that there are not more sick people onboard. Perhaps some of the ultra-Orthodox Jews are reluctant to take medicine from a Palestinian doctor, fearing that he might offer them drugs that can harm rather than help them. An insulated community, they rarely accept help from outsiders.

Giving us medicine is paradoxical. After all, it's being hostages that's making us ill, and then our captors' doctor comes to reduce our symptoms so we feel better. Most of our physical ailments would go away if we were just sent home. Of course, we're thankful for what the doctor is offering to those who are ill.

Halla summons me for a second interrogation and leads me to the first-class cabin. Halla's green eyes are dim, cloaked in a veil of melancholy. Bob heard from a crew member that her wedding was to have taken place on the day the Six-Day War broke out, three years ago, but her fiancé was killed in the fighting. In response, Halla dedicated her life to the liberation of Palestine from Israeli oppressors. Other members of her family are equally committed to the movement, and several are imprisoned in Israel because of their affiliation with the PFLP.

In other words, she already hates me for having that medal that represents the loss of her fiancé just three years ago.

I sit in the same seat in the first class cabin I was in yesterday. The interrogator is the same man—the one with the jagged scar. Scarface begins with familiar allegations: I'm an Israeli soldier and a Zionist with dual passports. This time I feel better prepared to adamantly deny each accusation. I need to keep my wits about me and be confident to get through this.

"Tell me about your Israeli husband. He's also in the army? You met him during your military service?"

I am taken aback by this new line of questioning.

"*Husband*? I'm not married! I'm twenty years old. Single. An American college student. I *am not* in the Israeli army—not now, not ever. And I don't have a husband."

He turns and talks with Halla in Arabic, giving me a momentary rest from his verbal assault. I fear they are discussing the new so-called evidence they found today in my checked luggage.

"Stop lying!" he yells. "We have seen the pictures of you and your husband in your Israeli uniforms. It's time now to tell us about him, and your army service."

"No, I never served in the Israeli army. I'm American. Those pictures were of me and my friends. I don't have a husband, not even a boyfriend. That guy is just a friend, you know, someone you talk to and hang out with."

My temples are pounding, and a sense of dread is gripping my body. I've already lost my momentary confidence.

He persists. "And the medallion we found in your suitcase? Why do you have that if you are not proud of the Six-Day War? Where were you and your husband fighting? In Golan Heights? In the West Bank or Gaza? How many of my people did you kill? You and all the Israelis are the reason Palestinians became refugees. You and your people have ruined our lives."

The pounding is becoming stronger, louder, my head is about to explode. I close my eyes, giving myself a few seconds to pause.

"That medallion was a gift, a friend gave it to me when I left the kibbutz. I'm not a soldier—I didn't fight in any wars. I've never held a gun. I've never killed anyone, and I never will."

I try hard to keep my voice steady although I'm choking up. What is this "evidence" they are trying to collect even for? A burning sensation rises to my throat, and I think I may throw up all over myself. I swallow hard to quell the feeling, trying to calm my churning stomach.

"*You and your people are our enemy. We can find you wherever you are. You will not be safe. We have your passport and information about where you live.*"

A sob catches in my throat. Will I need to worry about the PFLP forever?

I tell myself these were empty words from a desperate man, nothing more. I'm tired of being accused of being something I'm not. I'm frustrated by my inability to explain myself. The interrogator's anger stings me like a swarm of bees.

Finally, when they grow frustrated with my repeated denials, Halla escorts me to my seat. I have no idea how long I've been questioned, but it feels like an eternity. Near collapse, I tell Mike about the new accusation that I was married to an Israeli soldier, with whom I served in the Six-Day War.

Mike has been interrogated again, too. They questioned him about his own military service, demanding details about where he fought and how many Palestinians he killed. Like me, he vehemently denied these allegations. Together, we ponder what all these accusations mean. It seems our captors are more aggressively targeting a few of us, including me and Mike.

I gladly take the cigarette he offers and focus on the smoke rather than on the tightness in my throat. Though I'm not really a smoker, I do smoke sometimes at college with friends, especially when I'm drinking. But now, we share our cigarettes in silence. Neither of us can bring ourselves to conjure any funny commentary. We are both startled by the new threat of being able to find me once I'm back home. As frightening as those words are, I need to believe there is also a ray of hope embedded within them.

It implies that we *are* going home.

DAY 6

TAKEN

About 3:00 a.m., two men with blinding flashlights walk slowly down the aisle. They shine the light at my face and at Mike, curled up by the window.

"Mike Shaw?" His body jerks awake.

"Yeah, that's me."

"Come with us right now. Quick! Put on your shoes!"

Mike bends over, slipping his large feet into his black Converse sneakers. His hands tremble as he ties his laces. I fold my legs tightly into my chest so he can get by. Mike walks behind the guerrillas to the front of the plane. I want to say something comforting to him, but I'm afraid to speak, and he doesn't meet my eyes. I can't see where he's gone, but I assume he's been escorted down the ladder like the men who were taken three nights ago. Am I too pessimistic? Maybe this is a middle-of-the-night interrogation, and Mike will soon return. But then why does he need his shoes?

Falling back to sleep is out of the question. Mike's presence beside me provided a feeling of protection from the armed guards who lurk about the cabin, and now, just like that, it's gone. The intensity of our experience over the last few days created an intimacy that transcended normal time. During the long, hot hours on the plane, we exchanged stories about our summers in Israel, reminisced about families and friends back home, and dreamed about traveling the world after college.

I told Mike all about Kibbutz Megiddo, where, while picking pears, I watched each day dawning, the rising sun casting a pinkish glow across the sky. He lit up at my story about the one sunset when I'd gone with a few other farm volunteers to climb up a rocky hill, Har Megiddo (Mount Megiddo), where we got stoned and gazed at the twinkling lights of the valley that stretched beneath us. It was the biblical site of Armageddon, where the epic battle of good versus evil was to take place. High from a couple of shared joints, our group of volunteers laughed about what the last battle might look like. Mike and I joked that smoking weed might help us get through the stressful times on the plane.

And now I am alone. I'm not sure how I'll manage without Mike; his ability to make jokes about everything was a familiar coping style for me. At home, my mother, sister, and I could often find something to laugh about, usually at other people's expense. It was a strategy to avoid talking openly about our deeper emotions. Without laughter as a buffer, my vulnerability and the dangers we face are painfully evident.

One by one, ten other men are escorted down the aisle: Bob, Ben, four young Orthodox men, and three older rabbis. Ranging in age from about sixteen to fifty, they are all Americans, and, as far as I know, except for Bob they're all Jews. I figure Bob is being taken because of the Israeli visa stamps in his passport.

Most of these men have family still on board. Young children sleep peacefully, but their wives and mothers are fully awake, like me. Some cry loudly, filling the otherwise silent space. Others stare blankly. Mrs. Raab, whose seventeen-year-old son, David, was removed from the plane, attempts to follow him down the aisle until Ramy fiercely orders her to sit. When she refuses, he repeats the command, pointing his machine gun at her chest.

"He's just a boy," she cries.

They ignore her pleas. She moves to the window at the back of the plane, desperate for a glimpse of David. But the night is black, and she can learn nothing. She gazes out for several minutes. Eventually, she hears her younger children calling her. She returns to her seat and tells them David is gone. She consoles them as they cry.

I reach for the pack of cigarettes Mike left in his seat pocket. I light one, then another, inhaling deeply and slowly. Smoking calms me. I lie awake long into the night gazing into the darkness, haunted by Mike's absence. I gather the energy to go to the toilet to change my tampon. The stench no longer bothers me; I am spaced out, numb, robotic in my movements. It's no comfort that I have more room now as I sprawl across the three seats in our row and stare at the gray ceiling.

At first light, I walk stiffly to the back of the plane, legs asleep, trying to jump-start my circulation. Rachel is awake, so I stop beside her. "They took Mike and Bob." She takes my hand and squeezes it. Touch is so important now; it helps me feel human in a time when life as I know it seems to be slipping away.

Rachel has also been interrogated twice, for a couple of hours each time. Because she speaks Arabic, the Palestinians suspect she's a spy. They have false "evidence" of her being an Israeli soldier—in her luggage they found a picture of her in a khaki army shirt holding a rifle, standing amid other soldiers. Like me, Rachel was just hanging out with friends, posing for fun.

Across the aisle, Hannah sits by the window with the curtain drawn, holding her radio unobtrusively to her ear. With the volume low, she strains to listen to the Jordanian national radio station. Although Hannah knows Arabic, she is trying to keep her knowledge of the language a secret. The Palestinians already know Rachel speaks Arabic; they saw on her passport that her birthplace was Sudan and asked her immediately about her language skills. She told them the truth.

From the news broadcast, Hannah learns the USS *Independence* arrived near the Lebanese coast that morning, possibly preparing for military intervention on our behalf.

"Well," she begins in a soft voice, "King Hussein and his government have little control over our fate. The Palestinians are only allowing the Jordanian soldiers to bring food and medical care, nothing else. If Jordanian soldiers try to free us, the PFLP are threatening to kill all of us. The king and his generals are pressuring the guerrillas to let us go—they're firing on refugee camps near Amman. The Palestine Liberation Organization (PLO), the umbrella organization for the Palestinian guerrilla groups, was also attacked."

We all exchange uneasy looks, wondering what else is going on that we don't know about.

Hannah continues. "I also heard the PLO wants to take charge and get *most* hostages released quickly. But here's the bad news—the PLO spokesman said they planned to keep some passengers—Israeli citizens and those suspected of being in the Israeli army. They're going to hold those people until *all* Palestinian prisoners in Israel are released."

I try to make sense of this new information. The prospect of a U.S. military intervention to free us is the best news I've heard all week, but the news about the PLO is confusing. What does it mean if *another terrorist organization*, the PLO, takes charge of our release? If the plan is to release all passengers except for Israelis and those suspected of being in the Israeli army, what will happen to me, Rachel, Shoshana, and others whom they believe are Israeli soldiers?

The PLO's intention to intervene does not sit well with our captors, the PFLP, who come on the plane that morning with their weapons, demanding we remain in our seats. One of the chief interrogators demands to inspect all the hand luggage again as well as coats and jackets in the overhead bins. Row by row, they order us to hand over our belongings. I shove the remaining tampons far down into the seat pocket. Everything else—my books, my contact lenses, my wallet—now seem less valuable than those four tampons, and I obediently hand it all over. A guard takes each bag and flings it out the front door. Another man ferries our possessions into the tent, where several commandos commence the inspection.

I can only assume they are searching again for Israeli passports or even pieces of them. Only with "conclusive evidence" of who is on board can they negotiate exchanges for their own soldiers in Israeli prisons. We watch in collective horror as three PFLP members attach wires—explosives—to the outside of our plane as Halla shouts and threatens that they might be forced to blow up the planes—*with us still on board*—if their demands are not met. My heart begins thumping so wildly in my chest that I'm sure others can hear it.

It is clear to us that the PFLP are unwilling to cede control of their hostages—or the negotiations—to the PLO. It is their show, even if it means killing us all. The question is, does anyone outside of this desert runway understand that? Without Bob and Mike, I'm like a fish out of water, feeling alone and gasping for breath.

We haven't eaten breakfast, but most of us are too worried to notice or care about our rumbling stomachs. After what should have been lunchtime, the passengers in charge of food distribution give each of us a half piece of stale bread with jam and a small cup of heavily chlorinated water. One taste and I spit it back into the cup.

Midafternoon, a sandstorm with gales of wind brings drifts of fine sand into the cabin. The crew refit the doors quickly, but the damage has been done. Passengers cough from the sand-filled air. We can no longer see out the windows as the sandy dust clots into thick, low clouds. We can do nothing but sit in the gritty cabin, frightened and hungry in our sweltering prison. After the storm passes, the crew removes the doors, and we eagerly inhale the slightly cooler, fresher air.

In an attempt to conjure some quasi-normalcy, Rachel, Shoshana, and I again organize camp time with the children. Six kids join us. We make the most of the games we managed to save from the inspection: checkers, a pack of cards, and a book of riddles. When we're done playing, we move on to singing, closely following Shoshana, our chorus leader. After singing our well-rehearsed repertoire of "Old McDonald Had a Farm," "Up, Up, and Away on TWA," and "*Living* on a Jet Plane," Shoshana teaches all the lyrics to Julie Andrews's "Supercalifragilisticexpialidocious" and challenges the kids to remember the long, silly word and to chime in with the refrain, "um diddle liddle um da lie," repeated four times, to its catchy upbeat tune. Managing the tricky words is a new and fun experience for most of them.

The Orthodox women on board fret that it is Friday afternoon and the Sabbath—important to all observant Jews—is fast approaching. They ask the guards to bring candles for the Sabbath ritual. At first, the guards insist they have no candles, but when the women become more agitated and persistent, they eventually come on board with two. It's a small but surprising concession and, as the candles are lit, I reflect that this is not the first time the Palestinians' humanity and caring have surfaced. These are people who understand the importance of faith, who are now showing respect for rituals they do not share. It brings a glimmer of gratitude into this dark place.

Ordinarily, the oldest woman in the Jewish household lights the candles on Friday at sunset, reciting a blessing that welcomes the sacred arrival of the Sabbath. Tonight, the wife of a rabbi, the eldest woman on the plane, does the honors. She has a small bag of soup nuts (a crunchy garnish) from Israel, which she distributes in lieu of traditional bread to those who gather around her. This ad hoc celebration of the Sabbath ritual without challah bread evokes the memory of the resilience of Jews during the Holocaust who observed holidays with whatever small substitutes they could find.

Under other circumstances, this ritual is a comfort to me, too; candle lighting was something my mother and grandmother did together on Friday night just before sunset. I usually stood by their side as they covered their eyes reciting the prayer. Candles brought a sense of peace into our home, adding light and warmth to our surroundings.

Later, the family gathered around the dining room table, adorned with an embroidered tablecloth for the special meal. My father recited the kiddush prayer over a glass of wine, before we enjoyed a meal that included chopped liver, meatball fricassee, roasted chicken or brisket, green beans or other vegetables, challah, and dessert. I loved how the softened challah slid smoothly down my throat after being dipped in the fricassee. In high school and certainly now, away at college, I've rarely been home for these meals. But they remain deeply etched in the recesses of my memory, and I find myself longing to once again be amid those familiar Friday smells wafting through my parents' house.

We are pleasantly surprised when a hot meal is brought aboard. Passengers and crew pass out boxes of baked chicken, pita bread, salad, and a small box of orange juice. This time more of us eat, including some of the observant passengers. I wolf down the food and drink, not having had a substantial meal for what seems like days. My stomach has flattened over the past week, and I'm certain that I've lost weight. In my other life, the life before I was a hostage, the life where I'm an ordinary American college student, this would have made me happy. Such concerns seem so far away now, so unimportant given the uncertainty of our lives. It doesn't matter how thin I am if I'm dead.

Shortly after we finish dinner, all remaining men, including the captain and male crew, are instructed to put on their shoes and assemble at the front of the plane. The men are soon gone. Again, the distraught wives left behind worry for their welfare. But this time, those who are observant are especially concerned because their husbands have been driven away on a day when Orthodox Jews may only travel on foot. I shudder thinking about the other men who were forced off the plane earlier and driven away. Are they still alive?

Mike and Bob offered me friendship and quiet strength when I was dejected; their presence calmed me after my most frightening moments. Wherever they and the others are being held, I pray they are safe.

Now only women and children remain, about forty-five of us.

DAY 7

EXPLOSIONS

All week I've been catching my captors staring at me; my legs are easy targets in a short dress, and so is the rest of me, young and alone. I'm more vulnerable than many of the women on board. In Israel and in Morocco, I learned the importance of appearing modest at religious sites. Not wanting to attract attention at the Western Wall in Jerusalem, and the Souk Semmarine in Marrakech, I wore a long skirt and a loose blouse with sleeves and carried a big scarf in my backpack. On this trip home, I did not expect modesty to be an issue.

But now that there are no men left on the plane, a new layer of fear takes hold—that we may be raped or assaulted by male guerrillas.

Eight of us volunteer to guard the others, taking two-hour shifts at night, standing near the door. During my shift, I try to remember the men who brought candles to welcome the Sabbath, a reminder that kindness can transcend politics and religion.

Even if they have spent far more time interrogating and threatening us.

We have no actual plan should an armed commando attempt an assault. Maybe I'd be the first victim. Would he (or they) take me to a private place, the cockpit, or off the plane under the wing or in the tent? Would they rape me in front of the other women? I know I shouldn't dwell on these possibilities, but it seems wise to mentally prepare. Maybe I can lash out with available weapons, like a spoon or butter knife, or I can yell loudly to wake the other women.

Tampons aside, the stewardesses provide little support to the women passengers. At least that's how I see it. I'm sure it's been very difficult for them to be on the plane for six days, needing to oversee the care of the once-upon-a-time customers. But their seemingly friendly relationships with the PFLP raise questions. Maybe they're just cooperating to ensure that the guerrillas treat us as humanely as possible. I doubt any of the crew are Jews, so perhaps they are at less risk than the rest of us. Then again, among the men taken early in the week, several were not Jewish; perhaps they were of interest because of their work in the U.S. government or for other reasons.

When the sun rises and my watch ends, I head to the lavatory, grateful the night has been uneventful. Our diminished numbers mean there is no longer a line. Since there are only women on the plane now, I leave the door slightly ajar to allow some light. The squalor revolts me, and I change my tampon quickly.

Bettie and Mary scrounge up the last of the pita bread and jam from the galley, but there is not enough to satisfy our growing hunger. The stale bread is difficult to swallow with no water. I break the quarter piece of pita into smaller bits and chew well; I don't want to waste even a crumb. The sandstorms and shortage of drinking water have left my mouth parched and my lips cracked.

About 10:00 a.m., Bassam and Halla rush onboard and read a list of names of passengers who are ordered to come to the front of the plane. My name is not called. With little to carry but themselves, small bags, and their children, those called move quickly, hoping they are being released. There is no announcement of where they are going.

A line of women and children—perhaps forty of them—exit the plane. When I see the stewardesses at the end of the line, prepared to follow, I panic.

I count only five of us left. All Jewish.

"Please don't leave us here alone," I plead. "Rachel and Shoshana are only nineteen and I'm twenty. Susan is only sixteen. Mrs. Greenberg's name wasn't called either. . . . We're so afraid . . . all those guerrillas with guns . . . please, can't you stay?"

Bettie looks at me. Then she smiles, leaning in as if she were going to offer me a cup of airplane tea or coffee. "Everything will be okay. You'll be released in the afternoon. I'm sure we'll see you later in Amman." She slings her TWA overnight bag over her shoulder and walks off the plane without looking back.

I tremble. Fear and exhaustion are close companions now.

The five of us rush to the open door in the front cabin and watch despondently as the women, children, and crew board dilapidated vans. They start up the engines but drive only a short distance from the planes and then stop.

Rachel's face is pale. "Why are we still here," she whimpers, "when everyone else is gone? Maybe we should just get off the plane instead of waiting for them to kill us."

My stomach drops. Till this moment, Rachel's been a rock, a solid optimist. But she has a point; they've left the five of us alone on the plane with no guards, so what's to stop us from climbing down? Then I spot some armed commandos hovering under the wing; it's not a good idea after all. We don't want to provoke them; after all, the plane is wired with explosives.

Mrs. Greenberg is the oldest among our group. She seems steadier, perhaps because of her ultra-Orthodox faith. "We'll be in the second shift . . . you'll see," she says. Her husband, Rabbi Avrum Greenberg, was taken off the plane in the same group as Mike, Bob, and Ben, but she and I haven't really talked. In my experience, the ultra-Orthodox aren't interested in talking to women who look like me.

Even in the intimacy of our confinement, she still hasn't told us her first name. In our fraught and frightening environment, Mrs. Greenberg seems intent on preserving the customary formality among observant married women. This is not unlike my two grandmothers, who, despite their lifelong friendship, always referred to each other as Mrs. Beeber and Mrs. Barmat, never allowing themselves to address one another with familiarity.

"What about the other jets?" I wonder aloud. "Are those passengers getting off, too?" Susan and Mrs. Greenberg walk to the rear of the airplane to get a better view. They report that passengers are deplaning from the BOAC jet and walking toward the Swissair plane.

Devoid of adult passengers and the chatter of children, our plane falls eerily quiet. In the sudden stillness, I sense the shadows of their beings and the echoes of their voices.

We wait for a half hour, looking out on the desert, trying to understand what's going on. The bus with the other women passengers leaves Revolution Airport. I can only assume they are headed toward Amman, toward freedom. And us—are these our final moments? Will they blow up the planes with us on them, as they've threatened? These are horrifying thoughts, but I can't stop the reel. Over the last week—though it seems like a lifetime—I've become accustomed to not having control of my life, to not knowing what comes next, to thinking the worst while clinging to a shred of hope. That's what it means to be a hostage.

Then, from across the desert, more buses speed toward us, clouds of sand swirling in their wake. They park near the planes. Bassam barrels up the ladder and orders us to leave the plane. Relieved—though we have no idea where these buses will take us—we descend the rickety ladder for possibly the last time.

We're directed to one of the newly arrived buses, and once the five of us are seated inside, we are driven the short distance to the Swissair plane, where passengers huddle under the wing. Seventeen of the men are directed to board our bus; the remaining passengers get into other buses. I'm in no mood for pleasantries; I acknowledge the men who have boarded with a simple nod. We're quiet on the bus, all overcome with worry and fear about what will happen next and where we are being taken.

When we finally move, we drive only a short distance that gives an unobstructed view of the planes. We watch as our captors work intently and rapidly to attach wires to the sides and bellies of the aircraft. This seems like it can only be more explosives; men on our bus with military experience concur. One of them says they are getting ready to blow up the planes. I gasp with momentary relief, thankful we are no longer on them.

When the devices are securely in place, the guerrillas ignite the fuses, leap back, and run to the buses. My eyes are glued on the planes. I am caught in this frenetic moment, frightened, praying we're far enough away from the impending explosions.

A guerrilla jumps on our bus. "Open your mouths," he barks, "it'll be easier on your ears when the explosions start!" He rushes out to be with his comrades. It's all happening at such speed. I see others on the bus crouching on the floor, so I do that, too. But with the first booms, I jolt up, opening my mouth and covering my ears. Something is compelling me to watch.

The cockpit of the BOAC airplane explodes in a thunderous boom; metal fragments hurtle through the air.

Another explosion. Wings, windows, doors, seats, propel upward and shower on the sand in fragments.

The ground shakes and rocks our small bus so forcefully, I fear it might tip on its side or flip over completely. Or maybe a flying shard from a window or door will hit our bus. But then I become so consumed with the explosions that I've numbed to my feelings and can no longer hear myself think.

In this moment, I'm a voyeur, bearing witness to the destruction.

Another boom thunders through the air . . . and the fuel tanks of our TWA plane shoot into the sky . . . followed by the fuel tanks of the Swissair and BOAC jets.

Orange and yellow flames morph into thick black smoke. Explosion after explosion, in rapid succession, each destroying sections of the planes. Thick black smoke balloons across the blue expanse of sky, leaving the beige expanse of desert far below. The destruction occurs with such force that I've been caught in the moment, a spider hanging motionless in her spindly web.

When the explosions stop, only the tails of the planes remain intact.

Ashes scatter in great heaps on the sand.

Now I'm aware of the acrid smoke stinging my nostrils, and the bitter, metallic taste in my mouth. My eyes are burning. There's a loud ringing in my ears. Covering them and opening my mouth did nothing to block the thunderous sound.

My tears, my fears, my screams were all swallowed for the sake of the others.

But the thick black smoke is seared into my memory.

I sit with my mouth agape. The planes are no more; they have been all but obliterated. Where there were three jets, one of which was our home for the past six days and nights, there is now only ash and clouds of billowing black smoke.

Our captors explode in wild cheers, hugging, screaming to each other in Arabic, and waving their guns high above their heads. Blowing up the planes is a blaring message to the world of what they are willing and able to do.

But what about us? How long will it be before the world knows about these explosions? Will they know we were not on board? And what will happen to us now?

Even as we breathe in the destruction, I'm still struggling to understand what they gained by blowing up the planes. It seems like little more than a colossal waste of millions of dollars. And for what? Perhaps my mind and senses are still dulled by the explosions.

SUNDAY NEWS

NEW YORK'S PICTURE NEWSPAPER

25¢

ARABS BLOW UP 3 EMPTY JETS

Because strangely, I share an aspect of the guerrillas' happiness.

Our stifling prison is gone.

I am alive, even if, little by little, parts of me have been taken: my freedom, my dignity, and my possessions. My identity as a young college student is gradually being eroded. But does that matter if I have my life? Could this be the end of our confinement? The small minibus holds the promise of freedom.

Within a few moments, Jordanian army tanks advance toward our buses. They were near the airstrip all week, unable to act. King Hussein's army is now in place and ready to free us. But, as the Jordanian troops draw close, our captors drag two men off our bus and hold guns to their heads.

Bassam jumps from our bus. The blue veins bulging from his forehead reveal his fury. He yells to the Jordanian soldiers in Arabic.

"What's he saying?" I ask Rachel.

"If the king's army doesn't withdraw, the PFLP will kill all of us!"

The standoff continues as Bassam argues with Jordanian soldiers. Rachel translates Bassam's final angry response.

"*One more step toward this bus and you'll return to Amman with only corpses.*"

A pang of fear grips my guts as my world spins in slow, sepia-toned motion.

Then, the Jordanian army slowly withdraws. I know they are saving our lives, but it doesn't feel that way. It feels as if they are leaving us to the guerrillas' mercy.

And I'm not sure the guerrillas have much mercy left. I'm not sure of anything now. All I know is I'm still breathing, even if it's toxic air.

The buses start up their engines and head away from Revolution Airport. As we careen across the desert, I take a deep breath, relieved but deeply shaken that we have managed to escape the standoff. Because

---

FIG. 7. (*opposite top*) Newspapers around the world carried stories about the detonation of the three planes. From the PBS American Experience video *Hijacked* (2006).

FIG. 8. (*opposite center*) The explosion of the planes begins. Pieces of the plane fly into the sky. From the PBS American Experience video *Hijacked* (2006).

FIG. 9. (*opposite bottom*) Members of the PFLP rejoicing atop the remnants of the airplanes they had just blown up. AP photo.

while we still don't know where we're headed, it's clear we're not being released. At least, not quite yet.

The ride is rough across the pitted sand, and we bob on the hard seats. All the windows are open and, despite our attempts, we can't close them. People who have jackets or sweaters pull them over their faces. I have neither so I squint and put my nose in the crook of my arm to block the winds of sand that enter the bus from all sides.

The buses reach a paved, pot-holed road where crowds are gathered. I imagine these are Palestinian refugees who know the route of our buses and are waiting to bear witness to our ordeal—or their triumph. Women in long, loose dresses and scarves and men in baggy pants and long shirts watch from the sides of the road. Young girls move through the crowd, younger siblings on their hips. As the buses pass, more people rush out of their makeshift homes, cheering, clapping, and singing in support of the revolution and the revolutionaries.

News that the PFLP blew up the planes at Revolution Airport courses through the Palestinian refugee community. The black smoke, visible for miles, is a vivid demonstration of their power. The tumultuous outpouring of support for the revolutionary act chills me despite the heat, and I slide away from the open windows, fearing the crowds might charge our bus, seeking to harm us.

After about forty minutes the convoy nears Amman, and the buses in front turn to the right; our minibus veers to the left. Rachel, reading a road sign, says the other buses are driving to the center of Amman, but there is no sign indicating where we are going.

When we reach the outskirts of a town, our bus parks near a concrete one-story building. A throng of people circle our vehicle, their hands reaching through the windows. Women, men, and children—whole families—appear to have gathered. I am afraid to look for too long, not wanting to catch anyone's attention. The crowd, so large and agitated by our arrival, seems big enough and strong enough to overturn the bus as they lean into the windows and push on the doors.

An armed guerrilla clears a path through the sea of people and orders us into the building. The entrance is not far from where the bus is parked, but being trampled by the crowd is a terrifying possibility. The angry throng shoves and pushes, their momentum forcing us forward. I protect my face with my hands, peeping through my fingers as I did as a child during scary movies. This is not a movie. As a New Yorker, I'm used to riding the subways from Brooklyn into Manhattan during rush hour, and I learned to rely on the motion of the crowd to get me in and out of the subway car. But the hostility and anger of this mob is nothing like the crowds on the train.

It's nothing like anything I've experienced before or wish to see again.

Our captors lock the door behind us and push us into an empty assembly hall. It's cool inside the darkened room. There are no chairs, so we stand clinging to one another in a corner. I hoped we might be reunited here with the men who were taken off the plane a few days ago, like Bob and Mike. They aren't here and I wonder if maybe they've been released.

A new man wearing a now familiar uniform stands before us.

He speaks loudly in English; his words reverberate in the emptiness of the hall.

"The demands of the PFLP for the release of our prisoners held in Israel, Britain, Switzerland, and West Germany have not been met. Your countries do not care about you. They have not negotiated with us. We know some of you are Israeli citizens, have dual nationality, or are in the Israeli army. Now you are our political prisoners, our hostages, and we will keep you until your governments have met all our demands."

My powerlessness burns in my stomach, emptying my body down to my toes. For the first time since the hijacking began, I burst into tears.

DAY 7

WAITING

I am hungry, thirsty, and exhausted from my explosion of tears, a physical mess of dirty hair, unbrushed teeth, grimy hands, and a week's worth of sweat. Rachel looks as bad as I do; her long hair is knotted and uncombed, her eyes puffy from crying. When she sits next to me, I reach for her hand. We are silent in our shared but separate pain.

I'm still not interested in talking with the Swissair passengers. I'm scared about what will happen to us next, upset that we are still being held here when so many women and children are being released. And what has happened to the men who were taken—my friends—Mike and Bob? I might feel a little better if we could be reunited here.

Seated on the floor, I welcome the cool concrete on the undersides of my legs. The floor is dusty and dirty, but it doesn't matter. I stretch my legs out, prop myself up against the peeling wall, and adjust my dress to appear as modest as its skimpy dimensions will allow. Before my cramped week on the plane, sitting in this position on a cold cement floor would have been uncomfortable, but now it feels luxurious to straighten my spine, arms, and legs.

The room is empty except for posters and photographs tacked on the walls. One poster is a black-and-white drawing of women, two or three abreast, marching forward. Each woman is dressed in the same gray uniform, a military jacket and pants, but unarmed. They all wear the traditional black-and-white scarf around their heads, though each ties it differently, some more modestly than others. The kaffiyeh conveys a message of solidarity among the women. They have their hands in their pockets and look straight ahead, probably at their leader. PFLP guerrillas in training?

One poster features a drawing of a dark-skinned middle-aged man, his scarf concealing his nose and mouth, revealing only his light eyes and dark eyebrows. He stands behind barbed wire, holding a rifle. In English, the poster reads: *He is Not a Terrorist, He is a Freedom Fighter*, and beneath that *The Popular Front for the Liberation of Palestine*. As a hostage, I know the PFLP only as terrorists. *Freedom fighter* sounds more honorable, but calling yourself a freedom fighter cannot justify committing acts of terrorism . . . or can it? A third poster shows an abstract painting of a young Arab woman wearing a gray robe that covers her whole body and head. Only the bright green rifle she holds is not abstract. *PFLP* is written in English along the poster's bottom edge.

Many images in the room threaten violence: guerrillas posing on tanks with guns and photos of Arabs killed by Israeli bombs. My best guess is that we are in the PFLP headquarters where the hijackings were planned. I imagine that photos of the blown-up planes, featuring the billowing smoke and the airplane tails, will soon join this gallery of triumphant feats.

There are also a few black-and-white photographs. I recognize Yasser Arafat, leader of the Palestine Liberation Organization, and Ho Chi Minh and Mao Tse-Tung. Che Guevara, a hero of the New Left, is also prominently featured.

The image of Che disturbs me, though I am unsure why. He is a mythical romantic figure, a fierce fighter who was willing to die for his cause. Since his death a few years ago, his face has been plastered on T-shirts and hats and worn by idealistic young people around the world advocating radical social change. But the gnawing in my stomach tells me there is something else.

And then a memory emerges, at first distant, fuzzy, and then in sharp focus.

I was on a first date with a guy named Rick. We'd gone to a party and stumbled back to his apartment drunk. I didn't know him well but thought he was cute. Over six feet tall, handsome and muscular, with a mane of long black hair framing a chiseled face. We'd been drinking that night, beer, mixed drinks, and I didn't hold liquor well.

As we made out on his couch, my head was spinning from the alcohol. I wanted to get up but I was pinned under him. I told him to stop, tried to push him away, but he moved fast, unbuttoning my blouse, unzipping my jeans. I tried again to get him off me, but he was strong and forced his way inside me. I lay there waiting for it to be over.

The whole time, a poster of Che Guevara wearing his black beret with the red star hung on the wall of Rick's living room, looking at us.

The symbol of leftist rebellion, a pop art icon, now a witness to my date rape. Afterward, I quickly straightened my clothes and stumbled out, feeling violated and dirty. At home, I took a long hot shower. I didn't want to talk about it to anyone. I didn't even tell my roommate. Maybe it was my fault for going back to his apartment drunk. In time, I tried to forget. I almost did.

Now, it's like Che is watching again as I'm violated again in a whole new way.

In the hall, we sit for an hour or two with two armed guards by the door. Even if they weren't there, I would be reluctant to leave. I don't know if the crowd has disbanded, and I feel safer inside. I hope, in addition to keeping us from escaping, the guards will protect us from the throng that gathered before.

Prior to the hijacking, I had never been singled out or persecuted for being Jewish. Why would I be when our family lived in a mostly Jewish neighborhood, and my early schooling was at a religious school? In the public high school I attended, we read Anne Frank's *Diary of a Young Girl* and Elie Wiesel's *Night*. But to me—and to many young Jews—the Holocaust was a terrifying nightmare from long ago in a distant place. It was not a topic discussed by my family or relatives, or even that appeared in newspapers or magazines. Occasionally, my parents spoke about relatives they had helped by paying passage for them to Canada and about other family members who had fled to South America when immigration quotas had not allowed them entry into the United States. My parents, like many American Jews in the 1950s and '60s, considered the Holocaust as something they wanted to leave behind. To be accepted in the United States, they needed to present themselves as assimilated Americans.

With today's heightened interest in stories from World War II, it may be hard to understand why many American Jews took such a closed-mouth stance, but the truth is survivors were discouraged from discussing their experiences—even with their Jewish relatives, who were not particularly interested in hearing their stories. And books on the subject I read in our school curriculum were not initially popular. Wiesel's *Night* was considered "too depressing" for an American audience and could not find a publisher for many years. Anne Frank's diary was made into a popular Broadway play in the 1950s, but it downplayed her Jewishness and did not address antisemitism or persecution—nothing that would upset audiences. Perhaps Jewish people were afraid to learn about the details of the Holocaust out of fear that "it could have happened to them." Or maybe Americans were not yet ready to dampen the postwar optimistic spirit that pervaded the country.

Many of my fellow passengers have been raised closer to the reality of persecution and immersed and defined by Jewish history and religious tradition. They better understand what I do not: From the perspective of our captors, Jews are not victims but are perpetuators of violence and aggression. To the Palestinians, the violent aggression by Israel—supported by Zionists around the world—has cast them and their families out of their homeland and made them refugees. For many hostages, the PFLP's perspective is rejected as flat-out wrong—a distortion of truth. I heard the guerrillas' reframing of Israeli history but do not know how to interpret or integrate this reversal of the narrative of victim and perpetrator.

As a child of the '60s, a member of the counterculture generation, I'm accustomed to questioning authority. In Washington DC, I protested and marched against what I perceived to be the major issues of the time, the war in Vietnam, civil rights, and equal rights for women. I didn't get involved with Israeli or Palestinian politics, and I didn't know anyone who did. I thought of Israel, and particularly the kibbutz, as socialist and progressive, a place where everyone worked for the community and reaped the benefits. But now, it doesn't matter who I am or what my politics are. To the Palestinians, I am not an individual but a representative of imperialism and colonialism—the very things I protested in the United States.

In Israel, I had been welcomed as a Jew, free of the censure I had experienced in my Orthodox Jewish elementary school. There, even my young friends had judged each other by how observant they appeared to be as manifested by dress and public prayer. At age thirteen, I rejected this climate and insisted on attending a public high school. To my surprise, my parents allowed me to make the change, though my sister had to attend twelve years of religious Jewish education. I couldn't yet articulate how my new relationship to Judaism would play out, but embracing the cultural aspects already felt more authentic to me than what I had grown up with. In Israel I had connected with something I had not consciously known I was seeking. There, I was not judged for not being a particularly religious, or even a practicing, Jew.

I'd felt welcomed and accepted simply because I was Jewish. I'd never been to a country where most people were Jewish, be it the storekeeper, the postman, or the bus driver. I appreciated that Saturday, not Sunday, was a day when stores were closed and public transportation didn't run. Judaism was a way of life, a lived practice. That felt more comfortable than how I'd grown up.

My present situation seems to be the exact opposite. As a hostage, I'm not judged either; not because I'm automatically accepted, but because I'm automatically rejected.

In the midst of this panicked fear of death and destruction, practical thoughts about my return home enter my mind. I am now one week overdue for my scheduled return home, days away from the start of the semester. I wonder how I will make up the classwork I'll miss, or if I'll even be permitted to enroll. Have my parents called the university to inform them of my unknown fate? Have they contacted my roommate, Karen, to tell her what is going on, or has she called them? Have my friends already returned to campus, and are they drinking and partying without me? Imagining my life back at college is bittersweet but helps to eclipse dark thoughts about whether I am ever going to get home.

I'm still doubtful my parents have received the postcard I wrote to them on the plane and handed over to the Red Cross. The representative assured us they would be delivered, but no one has offered any opportunities for further contact. Is TWA or someone in the U.S. government giving our families updates about our well-being? How could they even know our well-being, without taking the terrorists' word for it? I imagine my family members seeing footage of the charred remains of the planes, frantic to know what happened to me. I have so many questions but no answers.

In that empty auditorium, disoriented and alone, we've heard nothing about what our government is doing to get us released. If they are still planning to rescue the hostages, could they even find us anymore? We have already traveled far from the site of the demolished planes, and we suspect they don't plan to keep us here, either.

PART 2

DAY 7

ON THE MOVE

We wait for hours in the dilapidated PLFP headquarters, fearful and bored, sometimes talking, sometimes silent. I still have no information about my friends from the plane, Mike, Bob, and Ben, and the other men who disappeared. Most of us remain sitting on the floor, but several men from the Swissair plane pace, lighting cigarette after cigarette, their smoke filling the room. I don't bother talking to them. I'm exhausted and have little energy to interact with those who might soon be gone.

The air shifts when a commando rushes in. "Hurry up, you're leaving. Bring everything with you!"

I shoot a raised eyebrow at Rachel and, seeing her grin, know she shares the absurdity of his order. We have little to bring with us. I have a small backpack, though most of its contents have been confiscated by the PFLP or blown up. Others seem to be in the same situation. I'm not sure what they did with our luggage after the inspection; one of the TWA passengers said they saw our bags being put in the back of a pickup truck the day before the explosions. I don't know if that's true or not, but I'm not concerned about my things. It's me—us—I'm worried about.

We hostages—five women and seventeen men—are hustled to the door. I'm hoping it's dark outside so we won't have to interact with the mob again.

The street is mercifully empty; only our minibus is parked by the side of the road.

On the plane, Mike and I joked that the hijackings were probably front-page news on the day they occurred but by now were old news, hardly worth reporting. But the fact was there was continued global concern for our safe return. While we were waiting through long, restless days at Revolution Airport, many world leaders consulted with U.S. officials to strategize a resolution to the unfolding crisis. Ambassadors from ten Arab countries condemned the hijackings as "savage and inhumane." When I learned this later, it contradicted my naive, simplistic belief that *all* Arabs hated *all* Jews and would support terrorist acts against us. Before the hijacking, I'd never understood the nuanced and complex relationships that exist across ethnic and cultural groups. Now I have no choice but to look for the nuance, keep hope, and survive.

As the days passed, we did not, in fact, fade from the headlines. Quite the opposite: international concern for our fate grew. The pope pleaded for our release. Even pro-PFLP Iraq and Syria advocated for our safe return. The United States sent six Air Force transport planes to Turkey in case immediate evacuation from Jordan became necessary. Nixon condemned the terrorists and announced an anti-hijacking plan, which included stationing armed guards on most American overseas flights and installing metal detectors at airport gates to protect against guns and bombs.

After the planes were blown up, while we navigated the mob and the time at the PFLP headquarters and now this second attempt to move us to another location, Israeli soldiers rounded up 450 Palestinians from the West Bank and the Gaza Strip, including relatives of one of the PFLP leaders. Israel claimed the arrests were "routine" and those detained were collaborators or members of the PFLP. Israeli newspapers called for the death penalty for PFLP members, identical to the punishment for Nazi war criminals. At the time, of course, we knew none of this. But we experienced the results: The Israeli government's response to the PFLP infuriated the guerrillas.

Back on the buses that brought us here, we settle into our seats accompanied by two armed guards and a driver, who immediately sets off through the town. We pass one- and two-room flat-roofed concrete homes, built side by side up steep hillsides. Many of the structures look like permanent houses. Others are makeshift: wood slats nailed together and to the sides of a house, sheets of corrugated tin weighted, with old tires, against rain or wind. There are few trees and little vegetation. Goats graze in narrow alleys. Clothing hangs haphazardly on sagging ropes.

About thirty women and children wait in line at a roadside water tap. Empty aluminum and plastic water jugs rest on the ground. It's obvious they have no running water in their homes, probably no toilets either. The women lift their filled jugs to their covered heads and scurry up the hills with their children, who carry what they can. From their clothing—

long dresses and scarves covering their hair—I guess this is a Palestinian refugee camp, though not enclosed by walls or fences. The community is densely populated. Have they lived here since the formation of Israel in 1948? Could they have lived like this for that many years? Or might they have come here more recently, after their defeat in the Six-Day War?

Once again, I have no answers to my many questions. By now, I know it's better to stay grounded in the moment. Looking out the window, imagining what other people's lives are like, provides me a brief respite from my own fear and anxiety, momentarily blocking the gnawing sensation in my stomach. There is little to say now as we wait, not knowing what the next hours hold for us.

About a mile down the two-lane road, we reach another community, this one with slightly larger houses with barred windows. The area is urban and, reading the signs, Rachel reports we're in Amman. Dilapidated two- and three-story buildings dot either side of the road with small shops selling canned food, sacks of rice, wheat, and vegetables. The neighborhood is crisscrossed with narrow passageways and twisted alleys reminiscent of the Moroccan town of Essaouira, where just ten months ago, I wandered its curved cobblestone streets and white arched walkways with my camera. Under other circumstances, I would have enjoyed exploring these streets, taking photographs at busy markets, observing what people were buying and selling, and interacting with vendors. But right now, my reality is far from any of that. I can't imagine coming back here; all I want to do is get home.

My reverie is interrupted when the minibus turns onto a side street and heads up a steep hill. At the top, the bus stops in front of a two-story white building. In fractured English and gestures with guns, the guards marshal all twenty-two of us into a first-floor apartment. We traipse in grudgingly, dreading another confinement. The space is hot and stuffy, probably uninhabited for a long time.

A quick glance around reveals three dusty rooms and a kitchen, bathroom, and long hallway. Each room has a window with narrow iron bars. Once we've all filed inside, they lock the door behind us. I look out the window and see two armed guerrillas stationed right outside.

We try a few light switches and find the apartment has electricity—lights at least, no overhead fans. The only furniture is a single metal chair. Mohammed, a burly guard with leathery skin, moves the chair close to the door and sits down. I notice he has a slight limp and is missing one of his front teeth. He places his gun on the floor within his easy reach. If we had thought to escape, this route is blocked.

Even with twenty-two people crammed into this small apartment, we have more space than we had on the plane. One by one, we stretch our tired, cramped bodies. We have upgraded from an aluminum shell to a concrete one.

I'm one of the first to claim a turn in the bathroom, which has a small, gritty sink and shower. There is no showerhead, but there is a scummy blue plastic bucket with a cup hanging from the top. I resist my urge to fill the bucket, throw off my clothes, rinse the sand out of my hair and ears, and wash off days of dirt. Having neither soap nor towel nor clothes to change into, there is no point in washing yet, but the prospect of cleanliness seems near. There is only one spigot—surely no hot water—but the appeal of simple cool, fresh water is strong. I begin a mental list of our most urgent needs. I still have two tampons left, although my period seems to have stopped.

The bathroom has a small window to provide light even if the electricity goes out, a luxury after the darkness of the toilet on the plane. There's a brown, heavily stained squat toilet on the bathroom floor. I'm sure the toilet will soon stink, so I'm doubly grateful for the window. The week on the plane has turned me into a practical thinker, assessing and appreciating our resources.

On the wall is a spigot and cup for washing your soiled areas after defecation. I've used this kind of toilet in my travels in Israel and in Morocco. A locking door, a working light, and running water all compensate for whatever difficulty the toilet on the floor might cause.

Ceding my turn to the next person waiting, I see that the men are sitting on the floor in the front room, but I'm not ready to stop moving. I check out the kitchen: The shelves are bare. Two gas burners sit on a concrete counter. There's a small sink with running water. In a drawer is a tea strainer, and a few spoons and forks. We can take turns eating if necessary—assuming we have something to eat. I sure hope we do. We've been given nothing to eat or drink that whole long day, since the destruction of the planes.

An aluminum kettle and a large cooking pot sit on a shelf with several glasses. I rinse my hands and throw water on my face just as I've seen the other women do. I wash and fill a glass with water, which I drink in one gulp. I refill it three times and drink nearly as fast.

A voice in my head shouts "cholera," and too late, as I remember the epidemic raging in Amman. The Palestinian doctor who offered medicines on the plane talked about immunizing all of us but has not done so, and I am still unsure whether a vaccine would provide such quick immunity, anyway. What have I just done gulping all that water? I could have tried to boil it in the kettle, at the very least. Maybe I'm not that practical or resourceful after all. But it's too late to take it back now.

I complete my tour of our new space and rejoin the other women, who have staked our claim on the bedroom. The small back room is the right size for the five of us and offers a modicum of privacy. The room opens on to the hallway, allowing us to walk to the bathroom without passing through the other room, where the men will sleep. Crucially, the door locks from the inside, which we hope will protect us from potential assault by our guard or any of the seventeen men in the next room, all virtual strangers. Although we didn't talk about it directly, we have shared an awareness of the importance of staying safe.

In a corner are five rolled-up, frayed straw mats. We spread them out and choose our sleeping spaces. Sleeping horizontally, even without a sheet, pillow, or blanket, is a luxury. I wish we could sweep the dusty floor before we lay down the mats, but there is no broom.

We hear a commotion in the next room and venture to see what's happening. Mohammed and another Palestinian carry in pots of food, paper plates, plastic cups, serving spoons, and plastic utensils, which they deposit on the kitchen counter. Rachel, Shoshana, and I follow them into the kitchen and dish out the food—rice and some vegetable stew. We are careful that there is enough to go around. The home-cooked meal is piping hot, and the smell of fried onion, garlic, and parsley is delicious—definitely the best smell of the week! They also provide loose black tea, a large bunch of mint, sugar, bananas, grapes, and pita bread. It is a veritable feast for twenty-two hungry hostages, who do not know how long this house will be our home.

Three men from the Swissair plane distribute the plates and utensils as we all assemble on the floor in the front room. Over this hot, tasty meal, we finally exchange names and share what little we know of our situation. Ken, an amiable Vietnam vet, is the only American man in the group. He was on the Swissair flight, en route from a military posting in Europe for a vacation back home. Among the men, there are eight Brits, six Swiss, one German, and one Dutch citizen.

The only hostage who does not join us for dinner is Mrs. Greenberg. Shoshana tells me Mrs. Greenberg is a Haredi Jew, an insular group based in Israel and New York who look to Jewish law to guide every aspect of their lives. Mrs. Greenberg refuses to eat any of the food, including the fruit and pita bread platter Rachel has made especially for her. She sits on her mat, alone in the women's room. A dark brown skirt covers her calves, and her legs and toes are hidden beneath thick stockings. Her arms are fully covered in a long-sleeved nylon blouse with a high-cut neckline, and her hair is covered by a wig. The sight of her makes me sweat, although I respect her need for modesty. Mrs. Greenberg clutches a white embroidered handkerchief and cries. Her matronly demeanor makes her look old.

After dinner, Rachel and I sit next to her mat.

"Is there anything we can do to help you?" I touch her elbow to convey my sympathy, my warmth.

She struggles to get words out. "I haven't seen my husband Avrum since he was taken off the plane. Maybe he's dead, lying on the street somewhere, or buried in the desert. I have to know where he is and what's happened to him."

Her sadness is so profound, I cannot help but be enveloped. Over the past week, I have managed to mostly restrain my own emotions, but now I fear contagion, that somehow the intensity of her feelings, wafting in the close, stale air, can transfer to me. I cannot afford to be weak.

Rachel takes her hand and squeezes it. "I pray your husband is okay. I bet he and the other men taken off the plane are all together somewhere."

Mrs. Greenberg pulls her hand back and stares at Rachel as if she is crazy. "I've been patient and quiet. I can't wait any longer. I must see him now. I must know he is safe. My husband is not in good health." Then, in a heart-rending cry, she repeats her husband's name: "Avrum, Avrum, Avrum." She lowers her head to her chest and recites a Hebrew prayer, her body swaying rhythmically, as people do in synagogue.

My ears ring from her piercing cries, which linger in the shadows of the room.

"Do you want some water?" I ask, not knowing what else to say. At least this would let me escape the room for a few moments.

Mrs. Greenberg stares at me without blinking.

Mohammed rushes in. "What?" he says in a low voice, pointing to Mrs. Greenberg.

Rachel says in Arabic, "She's afraid her husband is dead. She's calling to him."

"Okay, okay." Mohammed's face shows sympathy. He tells Rachel that Mrs. Greenberg's husband is being held with the other men from the TWA plane in a nearby refugee camp. Rachel translates but Mrs. Greenberg does not respond.

When she finally speaks, her voice is hoarse. "I don't believe him. He's lying. I'll only believe Avrum's alive when I see him with my own eyes." She begins to cry noisily again, her wails echoing in the empty room.

Something must be done, and fast. It's probably dangerous to have loud noise coming from the apartment; it could attract unwanted attention. If Mrs. Greenberg does not see her husband soon, will she carry on like this the whole night? What will become of her? Mohammed apparently shares these concerns, telling Rachel he'll try to bring Rabbi Greenberg. Mohammed summons a replacement guard and leaves. We hear a car start on the street. For half an hour, Mrs. Greenberg sobs while Rachel and I try to calm her.

Then, to all our amazement, Mohammed appears with Rabbi Avrum Greenberg. Mrs. Greenberg's eyes are suddenly bright, full of new light as he goes to her side. Despite their joy at being reunited, there is no public display of affection between the couple. She does not reach for her husband's hand, nor embrace him in a deep hug, nor touch him at all. I know that among ultra-Orthodox couples, physical demonstrations like touching and kissing are expressed only when they are alone. (Although, in contrast, they are loving and affectionate with their children.)

The rabbi speaks in subdued Yiddish to his wife. He is smiling but disheveled, his gray beard and dangling ringlet sideburns, *peyos*, in need of washing and combing. His long black coat is wrinkled, probably from sleeping on or under it, and his formal black hat looks as if someone stepped on it, or it was used as a pillow.

For privacy, Mrs. Greenberg gathers her mat and moves into the hall, and her husband follows. We have many questions about where he was held, who was with him, how the others with him are holding up, and if he has learned anything about our chances of release, but we ask him nothing, giving them time and space to reunite.

Rachel, Shoshana, Susan, and I head to the kitchen, relieved by Mohammed's humane resolution of Mrs. Greenberg's crisis. We agree tea would clear our heads. I'd have preferred a cold Dr Pepper or a beer, but tea is what we have, and it's a sorely needed indulgence. Mrs. Greenberg's uncontrolled misery fried my already frazzled nerves. We prepare four cups of weak tea—having brought the water to a full boil to allay fears of cholera—and add mint leaves and sugar to each cup. What I really want is a Hershey's chocolate bar or some M&M's, but as I drink the tea, I'm warmed, inside and out. By the time I reach my mat, I'm certain, even without a blanket, I can face the chilly night.

Curled on the mat, I think about the Greenbergs and my own parents. Besides a perfunctory peck on the cheek, I rarely saw my parents hug or kiss. They slept in separate single beds. I recall a day, when I was thirteen, when I was putting polish on my friend Pamela's nails in her living room. When her father came home from work, her mother greeted him with a hug and a loving kiss on the lips. Surprised, I asked Pamela if her parents often did that in front of her. They did. My parents didn't hug or kiss me or my siblings much, nor were we encouraged to talk openly about emotions. I learned from my mother, my role model for secrets, if anyone asked me how I was, I should always say "everything is fine." Now, as a hostage, hiding and suppressing my feelings, even from myself, is a well-honed survival strategy.

I know I'll have trouble sleeping if family memories keep replaying in my head in an endless loop, the way they sometimes do. I need a good thought, a soothing thought, to replace it. I think of Mohammed. Yes, he is our guard, stationed at the door with a gun to keep us from escaping. Maybe he would shoot us if we tried to leave. But he is also a compassionate man. Had he suffered separation from his family? Is that why he brought the rabbi to his distressed wife so quickly? Or was it merely the need to avoid drawing attention to the house with Mrs. Greenberg's cries? Whatever his reason, I'm grateful that he has put aside imagined and real differences between us, embracing our similarities and shared humanity.

As I close my eyes, I remember the Sabbath candles brought by another sympathetic Palestinian to the women on the plane, similar to Mohammed's response to Mrs. Greenberg. The kindness among captors lifts my spirits enough to fall gently into a deep sleep.

DAY 8

NEGOTIATIONS

I blink awake and the black metal bars on the window remind me I'm in a new place. The other women are still asleep, so I move quietly to the toilet. No line! I splash cold water on my face, hoping some of the dried sweat and dust will dissolve. A tube of Close-Up toothpaste has miraculously appeared on the sink, so I squeeze some of the red gel on my index finger and clean my teeth. Totally inefficient, but the sour taste that has been in my mouth for seven days is finally gone. There is no mirror, for which I am thankful. I don't want to see how bad I look.

I head to the kitchen and find Rachel awake and putting on the kettle for tea.

"How'd you sleep?" I whisper, careful not to wake anyone in the small apartment.

"Bad, really bad," she sighs.

"Sorry to hear that. What's going on?"

"I'm worried about all of this. Sure, it's better here than the plane, but who knows how long they'll keep us," she says.

I almost say, "Everything will be fine, I'm sure it'll work out," but I catch myself before letting the familiar words slip. That was the phrase my mother would use. I don't think she truly believed those hollow words. It was one of the ways she deflected attention and conversation from a troubling situation. Instead, I offer Rachel a hug.

"We've got to figure out what's happening," I agree. "Maybe we can ask Mohammed for a radio or newspapers. He might bring them."

"Good idea," Rachel says. "We'll wait till more people are up."

While we're drinking tea, Ken, the American guy, wanders into the kitchen. He looks every bit the soldier he is with his crew cut, tattooed forearms, and muscular body.

"How you girls doing this morning?" he says. "I'm thinking now we've got a group of seven Americans, we should write letters to President

Nixon and Golda Meir to tell them we need to be released. We're in a bad situation and these leaders need to help us."

"You think they'll ever see something we write?" Rachel asks. "A couple of days ago, we wrote postcards to our families and gave them to the Red Cross guy. I don't know if he came on your plane. I wrote to my parents, but I thought it was a slim chance it would get to them. How would our letters ever get to President Nixon or Golda Meir?"

"We'll send it to the American embassy in Amman, and they can send it as a telegram or read it over the phone to folks in the State Department. You've got to inform those high up in the chain of command. That's the way it works."

Rachel's voice becomes tinged with enthusiasm realizing the truth of his point: Our captors have no reason not to let us plead our cases. It will only help theirs. "Rabbi Greenberg could help you write the letter to Golda Meir," she suggests. "He's a Jewish scholar so I guess he's a good writer."

By now, the other men and women are getting up. Some wander into the kitchen, and others form a line for the bathroom, all of us adjusting to the new space. Two unfamiliar guerrillas bring bags of breakfast food into the kitchen. Rachel, Shoshana, and I—unofficially taking on the gendered role of feeding others—open the bags to see what arrived.

Susan—at sixteen, the youngest of the women being held—joins us. She was quiet yesterday but is slowly becoming more talkative. Ever since her non-Jewish friends were sent home, she's mostly been alone, like Shoshana, Rachel, and me. Like us, she has no idea what happened to her girlfriends, but we're hopeful they've gotten home safely.

We are delighted by pita bread, cucumbers, sardines, and thermoses containing sweetened black tea. Shoshana cuts cucumbers, Rachel and I prepare the plates, Susan pours the tea, and we feast in the front room. Rachel has prepared separate plates for the Greenbergs, and we're happy to see them eating the cucumbers and bread.

While we are cleaning the kitchen, a female PFLP member comes in and introduces herself in English. She's dressed in khakis and has a loosely tied red-checked scarf around her head.

"I'm Laila. I'll be checking in on you from time to time," she says. "Are there things you need? I'll make a list and see what I can get."

I begin by rattling off the list I prepared in my head. "We need to wash. We'll need soap, toothbrushes and toothpaste, towels, combs, and toilet paper."

"Whatever you can bring, we'll appreciate," Rachel says. "We really need a change of clothes, like pajama pants and T-shirts." I'm desperate to get out of my minidress, which I've had on for eight days, as it is hard to sit and get up from the floor. In pants, I'll be able to sit cross-legged and move about easily.

We expand our list to include washing soap for clothes and rope to hang laundry to dry. Shoshana asks for sanitary pads. Thankfully, my period has ended. So much for the practical stuff. We also need something softer than the tattered straw mats to sleep on, blankets, and pillows. We don't want to ask for too much, and our list is already long. As Laila turns to leave, Rachel requests newspapers and a radio. Laila grimaces, and I suspect we're not going to get either of those.

Left alone, the American hostages huddle on the floor to draft the letter Ken suggested. He and the rabbi take the lead.

> September 13, 1970
>
> To the American Ambassador in Jordan,
> President Nixon, and Golda Meir,
>
> We, the passengers of the hijacked planes TWA 741 and Swissair 100 have, as of today, September 13, become political prisoners after a week of captivity due to the negligence and political paralysis of our government. The lives of women, girls, and men are literally in jeopardy every moment. We demand that human consideration transcend all other political considerations so that we may be immediately released and returned to our homes in the United States.

Susan rewrites the letter in her best penmanship and passes it around for signatures. If there is even a remote possibility someone in power will read our letter, I want my name to be on it. After my return, I would learn that this exact text had been sent as a telegram to the State Department from Amman. A copy of the telegram, faint and marked up, was forwarded to my parents during my captivity.

In the afternoon, the four of us women are sitting on our mats when Laila returns with another woman, dressed in a matching military uniform, Nadia. Nadia is taller than Laila, with black curls framing her round face. Both women carry stuffed burlap sacks over their shoulders. We're surprised they've come back so quickly and excited to see what they've brought in their Santa Claus–like sacks. Before our eyes is the path to cleanliness: two bars of Dial soap, five loosely woven cotton towels the size of large dishcloths, five toothbrushes and a tube of Colgate toothpaste, and five black combs, small enough to fit in a man's back pocket. Most important is a change of clothing for each of us: T-shirts and pajama pants. One-size-fits-all apparel, previously used. The pants are all dark gray, but the shirts are different colors: black, green, and white. At least we won't look like uniformed prisoners. As if there is anyone to notice.

Mohammed enters the room carrying five thin foam mattresses, and an airplane pillow and blanket for each of us. He exits, but Laila and Nadia stay. The door to the room is closed, which makes the space feel private.

"Some of our comrades told us not to bring you these things," Laila says.

"We're thankful you did." Susan offers her a grateful smile. She is already making use of her comb, slowly unraveling the knots in her auburn hair.

"Some comrades want you to suffer, the way we've suffered all our lives. There's no one we can ask for things we need, not food, not clothing, not water. No one cares about us," Laila says. "I'll tell you about our lives, so you'll understand."

Turning to Rachel, she says, "It's easier for me to talk in Arabic. I want you to translate."

I lean against the wall, propping my new pillow behind my back. The knot in my stomach releases. Now that I'm sitting comfortably on a mattress with women who don't have guns and want to talk, I'm ready to listen.

Laila scans our faces. Maybe she sees me in that momentary glance—the me who's a person, a young woman like her—but maybe not. In reality (I've been wondering what that is) we're not alike, except for our age. Her checked scarf has fallen farther back on her head, her black hair peeking out around her face. She appears younger now, less severe, a woman with a story to tell. Nadia sits by her side.

Laila begins. "I want you to know something about us, about our family, so you can understand the lives of the Palestinian people. Nadia is my younger sister. I'm twenty-five, Nadia is twenty-two. We've lived in Jordan most of our lives. Our parents were forced out of their home and land in Palestine in 1948 during the *Nakba*, the catastrophe that displaced hundreds of thousands of Palestinians. That was during the events that led to the founding of Israel, when Zionists occupied our land. Thousands of our people were killed and more than half a million became refugees in neighboring countries. Our family left suddenly on foot, running for their lives. They fled into Jordan with thousands of other Palestinians, crossing a wide river to escape from harm. My parents brought what they could on their backs and atop their heads, but their arms had to be free to carry Nadia and me. Nadia was only six months old. Our older brother, Ghassan, was seven so he helped by carrying a small bag."

She pauses for a moment as Rachel translates for us, a role that seems to come easily to her. I admire her linguistic ability; she moves adeptly between languages. I wonder if she has ever translated before. Listening to her translation, the story of their escape reminds me of stories of my own grandparents.

"Our family had lived near Haifa for generations," Laila continues. "Some were farmers who had nurtured their orchards for many years, growing olive, pear, and fig trees. Our parents had a small food shop in our village where they sold rice, wheat, salt, onions, and other provisions to neighboring Palestinian families. When the Jewish Zionists came in 1948, they stole our land, they stole our shop, they destroyed our homes, they killed our people and wounded others, including our grandparents. Soon after we fled, our father and his brothers tried to return to recover some of our precious belongings, our household possessions, our memories, our seeds, but they were blocked by the Zionist army. We are still fighting to return."

Laila pauses again, nodding to Rachel to translate. Rachel takes a few moments as she searches for a way to express in English what has been said. When she describes the Palestinians abandoning their villages, I remember a friend on the kibbutz describing ruins of a village she'd seen while traveling around Israel. Now I better understand why that village had been abandoned and other communities lay in ruin around the country.

I shift my position on the thin mattress and take a big gulp of water. After feeling parched for days on the plane, I welcome this simple pleasure. Thankfully, even after gulping tap water, my stomach has been okay. Since then, we've been boiling all our drinking water, which we get from the tap.

Laila continues, "When we first came to Jordan, the five of us lived in a small tent, in a large refugee camp outside Amman. We had no running water or toilets. We had no land to farm. Now, the five of us live in a concrete three-room house. We went to school with other Palestinian children, where we learned English. We have grown up hearing about the pains, struggles, and joys of our parents and ancestors, and the beauty of our homeland."

I do some quick math. If Nadia was six months old when they left Palestine, then Laila would have been three. Neither of them would remember the land at all, but their family has kept the memories alive.

"There is no future for us in Jordan," Laila explains. "It's been hard for us to find work; there are few jobs for women. My sister and I joined the Al-Fatah youth brigade—the Palestinian National Liberation Movement—in our early teens. We were proud to wear the uniform of the children's militia, khaki pants and green army shirts. We had guns in our hands before we were sixteen. We learned how to use AK-47 rifles and explosives. Now we educate other women about Palestinian politics, mobilizing and recruiting them to join the PFLP. We are dedicated to winning back our homeland—what is rightfully ours. No matter what it takes."

Rachel's voice trembles as she translates. It is painful to hear about the hardships of the Palestinians. This is the first time I've heard Middle East history discussed in such personal terms and from a non-Israeli perspective. Their story emerges as vivid and real. Though I knew about the creation of Israel in 1948, I did not know details about the exodus of the Arab population during that time—how they were forced to flee—or that they still live in substandard refugee camps. Even now, I get chills thinking back to that conversation, knowing that this situation still persists, unresolved, today.

Our attention is diverted by a knock at the door. Mohammed enters and says some things I don't understand to the sisters, and suddenly they prepare to leave.

"We'll try to come back tomorrow," Laila tells us.

Sitting quietly, I ponder what I've heard. The expulsion of Laila's family from Palestine puts me in mind of my grandmother's escape from Romania in 1914. In Eastern Europe, Jews were allowed to live only in small villages, shtetls, under harsh and exclusionary laws. Grandma Etel and her three sons, aged seven, nine, and eleven, fled in the dark of night from their shtetl, to avoid border guards. The middle son, Moishe, later known as Morris, was my father. They carried little more than food for their journey and a change of clothes to the port of Rotterdam in Holland. There, they and other emigrating Jews crammed into steerage in a transatlantic vessel, where they remained during the eight-day passage to New York. It was there at the harbor that Etel and her sons reunited with their father (my grandfather), who had arrived two years earlier. He had learned English and worked in a shoe factory. Grandma Etel spoke only Yiddish and had never been to school.

My grandparents fled to a distant country in search of a better life, envisioning a bright future through hard work and schooling. They never wanted to return. In contrast, Laila's family was forced from their land and desperately long to return. As refugees in Jordan, Laila's family and other Palestinian refugees had limited opportunities for education and employment, unlike my father's new childhood home in New York. And, while Laila and Nadia grew up with stories of their ancestral home in Palestine, my grandparents hardly spoke of their past.

It's hard to know what to say after Laila and Nadia leave. It's a complicated thing sympathizing with the people responsible for your own misfortune.

We find the others sitting on the floor in the front room, eating pita bread with sardines, cucumbers, and tomatoes. After days of sporadic meals, I'll gladly consume whatever they bring.

While we are eating, one of the British hostages, named Malcolm, speaks up. "A few of us took showers when you were talking to those women. We've got towels and toothbrushes. It's your turn now, ladies."

I don't need to be told twice. Thrilled at the thought of washing my body, I swallow my last bite and grab my towel, the ladies' bar of soap, and my change of clothes. Locking the bathroom door behind me, I pull off the dress and underwear I've been wearing for eight days and toss them on the floor. There are no hooks to hang them on, and I want nothing more to do with them.

Waiting for the bucket to fill, I savor being naked and alone. I pour water on top of my head with the grimy plastic cup; it isn't as cold as I expected. I wash my body and hair with the sweet-smelling soap, bathing quickly with the one bucket to ensure there'll be water left for the others. The water that runs off my body is a brownish color from the sandy coating that settled on my skin.

When finished, I feel like my clean American self. The mini towel works surprisingly well for drying off, and I put on my new clothes. I'm grateful for the roomy pajama pants and the large T-shirt. I can't bear to put on my dirty bra, so I roll it up with my dress, hoping I'll be able to wash my clothes later in the day.

"How was it?" Susan asks. She gives me a once over. "Looking good!"

"You're gonna love it. I feel better than I have all week. The water's cold but not freezing. Go for it."

I sit on my mattress cross-legged, relieved not to have to adjust my short dress. I comb my hair and decide to let it dry before putting it in braids. It's hot in the apartment, but nothing compared to the plane.

Rachel is on her mattress, propped up by her elbow. "You look clean and a lot happier," she says. Shoshana agrees.

"Yeah, that's how I'm feeling. Lighter inside and out. Life's easier here than it was on the plane, but I guess that's not saying much." I don't say it, but I worry that all the things they've brought us are a sign that they plan to keep us for a long time. That's all I've got to go on: hunches, guesses, and imaginary endings.

"Anything would be better than the plane," Rachel says. "But now I can't stop thinking about Laila and Nadia's story and my own parents. We left Sudan to flee antisemitism and came to the U.S. for a better life. What happened to Laila and Nadia's family and other Palestinians is tough and I feel for them. But there's nothing *we* can do about that. They shouldn't blame us, but I feel that they hold us responsible for their hardships."

"I know what you're saying. I kept thinking about my grandparents and how they came to America," I say. "That's the story of so many Jews—running from persecution to find a safer place. But the PFLP don't see us that way. To them, we represent everything they hate, everything that was taken from them. I guess they can't see us any other way."

"Let's not forget how much Jews have suffered," Shoshana interjects. "We've got to look out for ourselves. Jews needed a safe place to go after Hitler's death camps killed so many of us. But now, years later, PFLP members like Laila and her sister want vengeance. I could hear it in her voice and see it in her eyes."

Susan returns from her bath, her hair wrapped in a small towel. "I feel great!"

"My turn," says Rachel.

I'm relaxing on my mat, drowsy now that I'm clean and warm. I wonder what I might have felt or done if my family had been forced out of their homeland.

The next thing I know, Shoshana is nudging me awake. "Time to wake up, sleeping beauty! You've been asleep for two hours."

"Did I miss anything?" I ask, sitting up.

"Nothing's going on, thank goodness. But they just brought food for dinner, so I thought you'd want to get up," Shoshana says. "Could use your help in the kitchen."

Dinner is, by my new standards, another feast. We cut up vegetables, cook them with rice, and serve them with sweet mint tea, and grapes for dessert. We put some aside in case this is the last meal they bring us. But as I'm well-rested and well-fed, and with no guerrillas around pointing guns, it occurs to me that I feel good—at least, as good as I can—given the circumstances.

DAY 9

RISING TENSIONS

The next day, after breakfast, we take turns washing our filthy clothes in the bucket. My minidress, bra, and underwear turn the water a disgusting muddy brown, the accumulation of nine days of body grunge, sweat, and dust storms. I scrub and rinse until my clothes are clean. There is no place to hang my clothes, so I lay them on my thin mattress to dry, the only space I can call my own.

Midmorning, Laila and Nadia return. We gather in a circle on the floor, facing the two sisters. Nadia makes friendly small talk in English. "You all look better today. You're lucky you have water, electricity, and a toilet, where you wash and change clothes. Many Palestinians in the refugee camps get water from a community tap, where they have to wait for hours and use the few public toilets we share with other families."

Rachel responds with a certain formality. "We're thankful for the clean clothes, food, and tea that you've brought."

Laila lights a filtered cigarette. Turning to Nadia, she says, "We can't stay long so let's get started." She passes her cigarette to Nadia, who takes a drag.

"Rachel, please translate for me," Nadia says. "Yesterday, Laila talked to you about our family. Today, I'll talk about the PFLP and who we are. But first, we've brought each of you a special book."

She takes four copies of a book from a burlap bag and holds one up, so we can see the cover. The title, *In Time of War: Children Testify*, is written in English. Nadia opens and turns the book around so we can see the pictures. I feel like a toddler at story time.

"The book was created by a Jordanian artist, Mona Saudi, who's been active in the Palestinian cause. It's full of drawings by Palestinian children. Mona gave school-aged kids paper and colored pencils so they could draw pictures of their everyday life."

Nadia pauses for Rachel to translate then continues to turn the pages, giving us a few minutes to absorb the pictures.

"You can look at the book later, but I want to show you something. Every picture tells a story of violence: airplanes dropping bombs, army tanks, and dead people lying in the street. That's their life. That's what our Palestinian children know. Imagine yourself as one of them."

It is easier to look at Rachel than at Nadia, who glares at us. There's an edginess to Nadia that is disturbing—I can sense her dislike of us. Though I didn't know it at the time, the Marxist-Leninist PFLP was the most radical Palestinian resistance group and one of the largest, with more than three thousand fedayeen, soldiers who pledge to fight till their death. In Arabic, Nadia begins talking about the movement.

"The PFLP believe violence is a necessary step in the liberation of Palestine. We're fighting a people's guerrilla war, so we must organize the Palestinian population. We hijacked and blew up the planes to shock the world and call attention to our suffering. Otherwise, we are ignored. Israel is not our only enemy—we are against all imperialists around the world who finance Zionism."

The PFLP had been founded just two years earlier, in 1968, by two doctors, Dr. George Habash and Dr. Wadi Haddad. Both men were Greek Orthodox Palestinian Christians who had received their medical degrees at the American University of Beirut. The two men became friends working in Palestinian refugee camps in Amman after medical school.

This information forced me to revise my assumption that the longstanding problems in the Middle East are solely a conflict between Jews and Muslims. In fact, a minority of the Palestinian population are Arab Christians, including the two radical PFLP founders. And was my limited understanding really any different from the guerrillas' assumption that most Jews are Zionists?

Nadia drinks a glass of water and nods to Rachel while she translates. This sounds rehearsed, like a lecture she regularly gives to women. It's clear that anti-imperialism is a guiding principle of the PFLP, and it doesn't escape me that it's the same theme endorsed by the anti-war movement in the United States.

The one I've been a part of.

"Our struggle is to fight so we can return to our homeland, Palestine," Nadia continues, "so we are no longer refugees. Imperialist nations like

FIG. 10. Leila Khaled was a hijacker in the foiled attempt on an EL AL Israel Airlines plane. The two Palestinian sisters spoke of her with great admiration. Khaled remains a prominent voice for the Palestinian cause. From the PBS American Experience video *Hijacked* (2006).

the United States give money to Israel and support and enable their military."

Leila lights another cigarette and offers it to Nadia as Rachel struggles to find the right words in English to express these complex ideas.

Before Nadia begins again, I tell Rachel I've got a question. I sense the sisters will leave soon, and I want to get my question answered before they take off.

Rachel nods. "I'll translate for you."

"Can you tell us more about the role of women in the PFLP?" I'm not sure how Nadia will respond, but I'm motivated by a curiosity about female revolutionaries and how they get other women involved in the movement.

Nadia understands the question without translation, though she responds in Arabic. "The PFLP has developed a separate women's movement because in our culture men cannot go into strangers' homes and politically educate and enlighten women. But as women we can enter freely. Many Palestinian women have joined the movement. Others are now sympathetic to the cause. In the PFLP, women are fighters, organizers, and leaders. One of our PFLP heroes is Leila Khaled, the first woman ever to hijack a plane. She inspires us. Her brave actions tell the world that oppressed people like the Palestinians can resist by raising arms."

When the sisters have to leave, Nadia gives each of us a book. I'm not sorry to see them go, as my head is spinning from the dense and troubling narration. Why are Laila and Nadia taking the time to talk to us? Are other Palestinians talking to the men? I recall the poster at the PFLP headquarters that calls the soldiers "freedom fighters," not terrorists. I ask myself again if words and philosophies can change the meaning of actions.

"That was a lot." Rachel sighs. "I'm exhausted."

"Translating takes a lot out of you?" I ask.

"It gives me a headache. When I speak Arabic at home, I'm talking about family stuff. Those political words—*oppression*, *liberation*—aren't in my usual vocabulary. When I translate, I bring Laila's and Nadia's voices and anger into my head. And it's more than the words. I've got to concentrate on going between languages. People speaking Arabic see the world differently than people speaking English. I've never translated much before, and definitely not about subjects like these."

"Well, we appreciate it," Shoshana offers.

"The intensity in their eyes, the whole vibe—it's a lot to take in," I say. "Since we can't leave, we might as well learn something, I guess. This isn't the history of the Middle East we learned in school or on the American news, or what we heard in Israel, that's for sure."

I'm curious about Nadia's and Laila's personal lives. Are they married? Is it possible for them to marry, or are they married to the revolution? I still can't fathom why they blame us hostages for the plight of the Palestinian refugees. I wasn't even born in 1948, when the Palestinians were forced to flee their homes. And what are we to do with the information they shared? Do they hope we'll be vehicles for their message when we are released?

I don't say anything to the other women about how unsettling it is to be seen as a Zionist, which is not how I think about myself, even though I understand the sentiment. Nor do I want to be viewed as an American imperialist, a characterization that is unfair in light of my opposition to the war in Vietnam. My identity is tied to the student movement, not to my middle-class Jewish upbringing. But this is not the time to explore the differences among us, especially about Israel. We four women hostages have bonded as friends over the last nine days; we need to rely on one another for mental, and possibly physical, survival. Political differences on how we view Israel are immaterial. We must be a united front.

"I'm surprised they brought us these books," Susan says. "The drawings are heartbreaking. These Palestinian kids are so young. It says they're eleven and twelve years old."

Shoshana has her book open, too. "Look at this picture," she murmurs. "This soldier is pointing his gun at a man, and it looks like those circles are bullets going into the man's head. This one looks like there's a bomb landing on a woman's body. You can tell these are children's drawings, but the bombing and shooting at people is impossible to miss."

All that summer, while I picked pears at the kibbutz, fighter jets flying in formation overhead grew familiar to me. Their thunder made it impossible to continue conversations until they were well out of sight. At first, I wondered where the planes were bound and what their mission was, but after a while they became a daily feature of Israeli life, and I hardly noticed them. Now, seeing the Palestinian children's drawings, the old questions and new ones suddenly beg for answers. Were those jets on their way to early-morning bombings of Palestinian communities? Or were they reconnaissance? It had not occurred to me to ask, nor had anyone thought to explain. The children's drawings hint at painful and disturbing answers.

"Look at this one," Susan adds. I bring my attention back to the pictures. "It's a drawing of a car that was bombed. It's simple but you get the point. Read the caption: *A village in Jordan completely destroyed by Israelis.*"

Rachel pages through her book. "There's only one peaceful picture. I guess violence is daily life for these kids. Their drawings remind me of a book, *"I Never Saw Another Butterfly,"* of children's drawings and poems from a concentration camp. Few of those kids survived. The pictures and words from that book still haunt me, and I think these will, too. Have you seen it?"

I haven't—and now am sure I don't want to. Shoshana has. "It made me cry just thinking about the daily misery those kids had to live through," she says. "No child should ever have to see what they did."

We're finishing dinner and drinking tea when Mohammed arrives with a few English-language newspapers. Ken perks right up, thankful.

Rachel and I approach Mohammed, and I ask her if she can please translate.

"I've got a few things to say to him."

"Sure, no problem."

"That was kind of you to bring us the papers," I say. "Also, what you did for Mrs. Greenberg yesterday."

I think it's important to acknowledge his acts of kindness, and I value Rachel's ability to translate for me. Mohammed looks at me and Rachel, his eyes wide. He appears surprised we are relating to him as a person.

He speaks in Arabic and Rachel translates. "I could see what that woman was going through. I understand being separated from loved ones and how hard it is. When my family fled in terror to Jordan in 1948, I was a teenager. There had been terrible fighting in an Arab village near ours, and we had no choice but to leave. We left so much behind. My grandparents were heartbroken to leave the house they had lived in all their lives. I still have those memories."

Rachel and I exchange a look. We're starting to understand more fully that the Palestinians have families and generational histories full of pain, just like we do. Twenty-two years have passed since their exile from Palestine in 1948. Over those years, the anger and desperation of the Palestinian refugees has grown into a fervor for revenge toward many Israelis and Jews. They have a similar loathing for King Hussein.

Rachel speaks to Mohammed in Arabic, and I ask her what she said.

"I told him how sorry I was to hear his story. I also said how much we share, even though we're so different."

Mohammed takes a drag from his cigarette. He does not respond but Rachel continues the conversation, gently changing the subject to ask if he has children. I can tell she feels it's important to get to know him, to befriend him.

He smiles at the question. "Yes, four. The two older ones are girls, twelve and ten. The younger ones are boys, seven and three years old."

"Your wife must be a busy woman," Rachel jokes.

Mohammed cups the cigarette in his palm. "The girls are a big help to her. They bring water from the tap at the bottom of the hill, cook a little, watch their brothers, and wash clothes. Soon they'll return to school. The older one is clever in her studies." Another Palestinian enters and our conversation ends. We return to the other hostages.

Ken picks up an Arabic newspaper that was lying by Mohammed's chair. Handing it to Rachel, he says, "This will probably have a different report of what's going on. Can you take a look?"

Rachel studies it for several minutes. I appreciate what a tedious job she has, but I am grateful to her for doing it. "King Hussein says the situation in Jordan between his government and the guerrillas has reached a dangerous point, and there could be serious destruction of people and property," she reports to us all. "The king is taking action to restore order. He wants all Jordanian citizens to support him. The PFLP believe the king intends to destroy their resistance movement and are calling for an armed confrontation by all Palestinian forces."

"It sounds like a civil war is about to break out between the king's military and the Palestinian Liberation Movement," Malcolm says. "Or maybe the war has already started. Our situation is about to get a lot worse—and fast."

"It would be a good time to let us go," Rachel says, to which we all agree.

Ken is immersed in the English-language paper, the *Amman Times*. "It says here the women and children who were released two days ago from the planes were sent first to Nicosia, Cyprus, where they spent the night. The next morning, they were flown to the U.S. They've all returned home safely."

"That's great news," Susan says, her eyes filling with tears. I imagine she's thinking of her two friends who are among them. Relieved, no doubt, but also wishing she could be safe with them, instead of still stuck here.

We remain in the front room, exchanging sections of the newspaper. It is a good distraction. It is my first opportunity to read about what is happening in Jordan. Only a day ago, King Hussein was reluctant to act against the Palestinians, but his military commanders insisted he do so. Fighting had already begun in the northern regions of Jordan, and Hussein's government was no longer in control.

I don't understand to what extent the hijackings and hostage-taking have created this dangerous and uncertain political standoff. What I do understand is our immediate prospects have not changed for the better. If the fighting moves south to Amman, there is no telling what might happen to us. Still, with so little control of our situation, worrying about the future serves little purpose.

DAYS 10–11

DEPARTURE AND REUNION

Shortly after breakfast, Mohammed, with Rachel's help, tells the European men they are leaving the apartment. They ask where they're going but he doesn't say. In preparation, they change out of guerrilla-issue pajama pants and T-shirts and back into their own clothes.

Mrs. Greenberg, who has stayed close to her husband since he arrived, turns ashen. She touches the wall to steady herself. "If my husband leaves, I'm going with him," she says.

"I'll talk to Mohammed," Rachel promises. "Maybe they'll let him stay."

I appreciate her willingness to act as a go-between. At any point, our captors could become angry with her, but that possibility does not deter her.

"Ken and the rabbi are staying," Mohammed tells Rachel, who shares the news with the relieved couple. I'm thankful that Ken, a soldier, is staying with our small group of women, though of course I would rather we all be leaving together.

But he has not told us where the European men are going. The men are instructed to stack their mattresses and blankets in piles, which tells me they aren't returning. Is it possible they're heading straight home? Or maybe to a hotel, where flights will be arranged for them? Why were they chosen to leave and not us? Have their countries agreed to release Palestinians held in their prisons?

For some reason—probably youthful optimism—it doesn't occur to me that something bad can happen to them. We've already been hostages for ten days and they haven't shot anyone (to my knowledge), so why would they start now? I feel like they're going home—like so many others have.

A wave of jealousy washes over me. I want to go home, too; it seems unfair that we must stay here. I try to look on the bright side; if they're freed, they can call our families. I rip the borders of an old newspaper and hand the small pieces to the other women. We share one leaky Bic pen.

"Write down your name, parents' names, and phone number," I say.

I entrust the bits to Malcolm. "I hope you're going home. Maybe they're just keeping Americans. If you reach the UK, or wherever you're headed, please call our families. Let them know you were with us in Amman, we're in good health, and hope to be released soon."

Malcolm promises.

I watch as they walk out the door and cram into a small minibus parked just outside the apartment. There are seven of us left.

Our shared space, which was so full, is now disturbingly quiet. Since we were first taken hostage, so much of what we've gone through is about change and loss: loss of friends, loss of material goods, loss of self. In moments like this, it's difficult to stay positive. Not knowing filters through every moment.

Ken breaks the silence. "Where do you think they're going?"

Rabbi Greenberg, who's hardly spoken to us, says, "Maybe they're going to the Wahdat refugee camp, where I was held before I came here. It's just a few miles away. And maybe they'll bring the other Americans here, to keep us all together."

"Why do you say that?" Shoshana asks.

Rabbi Greenberg shrugs. I wonder why the rabbi has not shared this information before. He usually keeps separate, not only from us girls, but from the other men. He spends hours on his mattress, reading from his prayer book. At prescribed times, he stands and prays, swaying and bowing—davening—in the ritualized style of the Orthodox.

I can only hope he includes us in his prayers.

Rabbi Greenberg and his wife are wearing the same clothes they wore on the plane. Perhaps they feel uncomfortable changing into the simple street clothes the Palestinians have brought us. The rabbi is still wearing his baggy black pants, a once starched, now wrinkled, white long-sleeved shirt, and a large black cloth skullcap. He has finally removed his heavy black coat. On either side of his body, near his hips, hang two white knotted strings or fringes, tzitzit, which are stitched to the sides of his undershirt. Wearing tzitzit is a duty for men, who—when they glance at them—are reminded to follow God's commandments.

My father, too, put on a prayer shawl, a tallit, with tzitzit each morning while he prayed. Shortly after rising and washing, he prayed facing east, next to his bed. As far as I knew, he never missed a day, but I really wasn't sure since he spent Monday to Friday at his business in Philadelphia. Deeply religious, he admired the ultra-Orthodox, who devoted their lives to following Jewish law. When I was little, I occasionally attended Shabbat services with him. I sat next to him in synagogue and, bored by the rabbi's long sermon, played with the fringes of his tallit, twirling them around my fingers. He seemed happy when I sat next to him, as he usually went alone. My mother went to services only on the High Holy Days, three times a year. Her role, as she saw it, was to maintain a kosher Jewish household and to oversee our Jewish education.

Turning to Rabbi Greenberg, I want to ask how many men were held with him in the refugee camp. Was he with Mike, Bob, and Ben? Were they okay? I'm reluctant to ask, maybe because of the impenetrable barrier he's created by his silence. He averts his eyes from the younger women. Among the ultra-Orthodox, men and women exist in separate worlds and believe that interaction with women outside the family can open a man to temptation and sin. Glancing at one's tzitzit is believed to reduce temptation, guiding the wearer back to the right path of God's commandments.

We are the same religion, but our practices and lived experiences are so different that communication between us is difficult. Their world is not open to outsiders or non-Jews and seems to be closed even to less observant Jews, like me. I haven't forgotten how distant I felt from classmates at the Orthodox yeshiva I attended and how out of my element I felt.

Ironically, to our captors, we Jews are all the same.

After an hour, fourteen American men from the TWA plane arrive, including Mike, Bob, Ben, David, and others taken off the plane on Thursday night. The TWA crew, including Captain Woods, copilot Jim Majer, flight engineer Al Kiburis, and purser Rudi Swindel, are also with them. While I'd hoped they were free and safe, I'm both happy to see them and relieved they are okay. We've been apart for five days. I hug Mike and Bob; others break out in song to acknowledge our reunion.

As our celebration winds down, I notice that Bob and Ben look pale and exhausted, dark eyebags revealing sleepless nights. Captain Woods also looks haggard, tension etched into his forehead, his crisp uniform now bedraggled. His shoulders sag from the weight of the responsibility he's been carrying for the passengers. Now that members of the TWA crew are with us, I'm hopeful new lines of communication will open with the militants and our government.

"What happened after you got taken off the plane?" Rachel asks Ben. "We've been worried sick about all of you."

"They drove us through the desert blindfolded and brought us to a refugee camp," Ben says. "They put us in a small room with one barred window, no furniture. They didn't even want us to look out the window. We had to bang on the door and yell "water closet" to go to the toilet, which was a hole in the floor with a flimsy door and half walls. After two days, some guy came in who didn't speak much English. I gestured that I had family on the plane and asked how they were. He made sounds like 'boom, boom' and said, 'planes finished.' My heart skipped a couple of beats, thinking my family had been killed—all five of them. I collapsed in the corner."

We all gasp in horror. "I can't imagine how horrible that must have been!" Shoshana says.

"I cried when I heard the planes were blown up," David says. "My mother, my two younger brothers, and my sister were onboard. I kept praying and hoping they were still alive. Luckily, just then another guerrilla came in, who spoke fluent English. He told us the women and children had been sent home. *Baruch Hashem, Baruch Hashem*, that's all I could say."

"Baruch Hashem, Baruch Hashem," the others echo—*Blessed Be God*.

"I told the guerrilla in charge we couldn't stay in that room," Ben says. "It was too small. Some of the guys were feverish, and we needed a doctor. And we needed to change our clothes. We were caked with sand and sweat from the plane. I felt like I had the cruds. Thankfully, the Palestinian doctor from the plane came and gave us aspirin. That helped."

Bob picks up the story there. "The next day, they gave us access to the courtyard and toilet. They brought us a clay jug of clean water and a bucket to wash our hands. They brought food and a stack of used clothes, shaving gear, and toothbrushes."

"They did the same for us. Did they also talk to you about the PFLP?" I ask, thinking back to Laila and Nadia. "We had visits with two Palestinian women."

"Oh yeah," Bob says. "A guy with excellent English spent time in the courtyard talking about the Palestinians and their cause. But we'd decided as a group we didn't want to talk politics. We told him the world should live in peace."

I briefly wonder why the men decided not to listen to what their captors had to say. We women had listened to the two sisters. Not that we had much choice. Still, by listening I'd learned something about their lives and their movement.

Mike moves close. "Hey, how about a tour of our new digs?"

"That'll take all of two minutes. But for a cigarette, I'll do it," I barter, teasing. I haven't smoked for a few days, but it was something Mike and I enjoyed together.

"Okay," he agrees. "I'll share." The cigarette he takes from his pocket doesn't have a filter, but I've stopped being selective about what I'll smoke—or eat. Mike lights my cigarette with a wooden match and, after a couple of drags, I show him around.

"We're so close to the next house," he says, his voice low. "The bars on the windows would make it hard to escape. In the refugee camp, we had six guards outside. There's probably that many guarding us here, too."

"Escape?" I reply, surprised. "Wow, that hasn't crossed my mind. Should we plan a getaway, Clyde?" It's comforting, picking up the familiar rhythm of our banter.

"Sure thing, Bonnie." Mike follows me into the women's room, which is empty. We sit on my mattress, and I motion for another cigarette. It's always been easy for me to light up one after another when I'm around a friend who smokes, like my roommate back in college, Karen. With Mike, too, smoking together creates a shared, intimate space where it's easy to talk. I like that moments of inhaling and exhaling give me time to gather my thoughts before I speak.

"So really, how've you been?" I ask. "I was so freaked out when you got taken, so worried about you. I'm glad you're here." Mike deflects by blowing a chain of smoke circles upward from his rounded lips. His antics amuse me, but I want an answer.

His light green eyes glaze over with sadness. "It's been hard. Especially when we were in that small locked room. I thought I'd lose my mind."

"How'd you pass time?"

"We played cards, chess, and Scrabble," Mike says. "Two of the guys got creative. They cut up little squares for Scrabble letters with a Swiss army knife from cardboard they found on the floor. At first, we argued about how many points the different letters were worth in the game. We decided it didn't matter, since we were playing for fun. Maybe we can find the board and play."

An hour later, thirteen more men, all Americans from the TWA plane, arrive at the apartment. They'd been taken on the second night. I hadn't gotten to know any of them.

"Welcome!" Ben says. "Good to see you could all make it to our meetup! Where've you been?"

His seemingly carefree, upbeat attitude amazes me.

One of the men tells us they've been held in Zarqa, a town about twenty kilometers north of Amman. There's been heavy fighting there between the PFLP and the Jordanian army, and local people fled with many houses destroyed by bombs. They were moved to Amman at the last possible moment. Along the way, they saw roadblocks, armed guerrillas, and streets barricaded with piles of rubble.

We're worried by this news. We haven't heard shelling or bombing around us, and I pray it's not heading our way.

Now, instead of twenty-two people in the apartment, our number has swelled to thirty-two.

The newcomers arrange foam mattresses and mats on the crowded floor, and Mohammed brings extras. Those who have not been able to bathe before take bucket baths now. By the time we settle down for the night, it's late.

In the morning, I'm greeted by a line for the bathroom. I'm told the water's been turned off, electricity's been cut, telephone lines are down, and the Amman airport is closed. Life is about to get a lot more difficult. But I can only live in this moment.

When it's my turn for the bathroom, I'm enveloped in the familiar stench. Only a half bucket of water remains near the toilet, clearly insufficient for flushing. The luxury of washing and teeth brushing is over.

In anticipation of the cuts, Mohammed and other Palestinians have brought in food and jugs of water. But with so many people in the apartment, our supplies won't last long. Luckily, we'd saved some food from previous meals.

Rachel and Shoshana are in the kitchen emptying bags of our usual fare: sardines, cucumbers, jam, pita, and large flasks of dark sweet tea.

“We’d better give everyone less food, so we can prepare for whatever’s coming next, right?” Rachel asks. We agree it makes sense, though it’s disheartening after our three brief days of no longer doing without.

One of the new arrivals has a small transistor radio, so we huddle together to listen to the BBC. We learn that King Hussein’s army is patrolling Amman in armored cars, small tanks, and infantry with heavy artillery. They’re shooting not just the PFLP, but all guerrilla groups organized under the PLO umbrella. Their chairman, Yasser Arafat, has declared, “The Palestinian Revolution will fight to defend itself to the end and until the fascist military regime of King Hussein is overthrown.” The U.S. embassy has been damaged by a rocket, and all the embassy cars have flat tires from being shot with bullets.

“That sounds bad,” Rachel says when the broadcast ends.

“Yeah, it sure does, but civil war in Jordan is big news.” David tries to reassure us. “It may remind people we’re still here. We’ll be on the front page again.”

“Maybe they’ll decide to let us go now,” Ben suggests. “The war is at our doorstep, and if we get killed now, what have the guerrillas gained?”

Bob seems inclined to agree. “There’s another angle to this,” he says. “What will the world think of King Hussein and his country if we get killed? Jordan will look weak militarily and politically because they can’t control the PFLP and the other guerrilla groups operating right under their nose. It’s in no one’s interest to have us dead. I bet they’re figuring out how to get us out safe right now.”

In spite of their optimism, others among us are more pessimistic. We’ve been through so much already, it’s scary to think we could soon be in the midst of a civil war—worse yet, we might even be casualties caught in the crossfire. But we haven’t heard gunfire yet, so maybe we’ll be okay.

I want to believe that Ben and Bob, both older and with more political acumen than I have, are assessing our situation correctly. With our group reunited, I feel less alone, comforted in the presence of friends.

But I know that comfort can change without notice. It already has, many times.

DAYS 12–17

IN THE WAR ZONE

The next morning, I'm aware of a shift in the apartment. Others around me seem more on edge. Our three days of running water have come to an abrupt halt, and the electricity is off. I'm worried about the water we'll be drinking now. Where will it come from? We don't know the state of the cholera epidemic, but that fear keeps circulating in the group. Worse yet, in the distance I can now hear a faint, echoing crackle of gunfire. It's not constant—it's more like a slow wave of detonations, followed by a calming silence. But like ocean waves, the frequency and intensity changes throughout the day.

I don't know how far away the fighting is or if it's moving in our direction. Even though we've been surrounded by guns for the last twelve days, I never heard them fired. It was frightening enough to see soldiers directing their weapons toward us, but hearing the sound adds a whole new level of panic. Even from a distance, some of the men believe they can distinguish between the sounds of submachine guns, mortars, and shells, but to me, they are all just sounds of destruction. How ironic that the interrogators were convinced I was in the Israeli army. Not only have I never held a gun, but even the noises of warfare from a quarter or half mile away terrify me. I hear it mostly during the day; thankfully, the nights—at least for now—are quiet.

From a radio bulletin, we learn that King Hussein has declared martial law in Jordan and demanded that all militants surrender their weapons to the head office of the Palestine Liberation Organization. When they refused, the Jordanian army attacked all suspected guerrilla locations and imposed a twenty-four-hour curfew in Amman. Jordanian soldiers have been ordered to shoot anyone on the street and to destroy any building from which Palestinians are shooting. Despite these warnings, our captors are still fighting on the streets, apparently ignoring orders to surrender their weapons. Mohammed and two other men alternate between guard watch and fighting alongside their comrades in different parts of Amman.

The war keeps getting closer. We see little of what is occurring on the street as we mostly stay away from the windows for safety. When I do venture a look outside, I see black smoke filling the blue sky. The distance of the smoke and the loudness of the gunfire tell me how close the fighting is, or at least I think it does. It's just a way for me to assert some control over the situation—I really know so little about what's happening outside. Mike and I pass time playing Scrabble and chess, but our banter has become more subdued. Bob paces the room nervously. I worry about him; it's easier to project my concerns onto others' mental and physical health than dwell on my own.

Two days later—our fourteenth day in captivity—the war is at our doorstep. Now, weapons are roaring and rockets are exploding nearby, the din of battle erupting again and again. The stuttering staccato of gunfire is a frequent backdrop. The gravity and danger of the war cannot be ignored. We mostly sit throughout the day on our thin mattresses, the only space we can call our own. We are hypervigilant, listening carefully to the sounds outside.

The worst moments are when we hear the whistling—a high-pitched sound that grows louder and louder as it comes closer. When the artillery shell nears its target, the whistling stops—a pause a few seconds before the explosion. The pause is the most terrifying moment, because we never know where the shell will strike.

Each time we hear the whistling—six or seven times each day, maybe more depending on the day and where the fighting is—we dash into the narrow hallway and take cover. Drawing on his years in the military, Ken has instructed us that the hall is the safest place to shelter in case artillery hits our building. This happens more often during the day than at night.

In the hall, we crouch on the gray concrete floor and cross our arms over our heads for protection. Packed together like the canned sardines we are eating, we smell each other's fear and sweat and share our terror.

In these moments when death feels near, I silently pray, a foxhole prayer, that we will be spared. All around me, others are whispering their prayers, too. My prayer is an act of desperation, a leap of faith. I'm begging for help from a god whose existence I doubt.

After each explosion, I look around to confirm that we are all alive. When the danger is momentarily over, we file out of the hallway, hands on the wall to steady our trembling bodies and quivering souls.

Not knowing when the next attack will come has us constantly on the edge of fear, a fear that ricochets off the walls in our small, crowded space.

I have no idea if Mohammed and the other guards are still by our door. Even if they're gone, and we could venture outside, I'm not going anywhere.

On a day of particularly heavy shelling, we huddle in the hallway, uncertain if our house will be hit. I sink to the cement floor and wait, breathing deeply, trying to calm my shaking limbs. I know only one thing for certain; I don't want to die.

I used to think of myself as old—well, old enough to be independent and make my own choices. But as I face the possibility of death, I feel young, much too young to have my life end before it has really begun.

The floor shakes violently; it feels like an earthquake. Artillery destroys a house nearby, and ash and debris fly through our window.

We hear cries. How many adults and children around us have been injured or killed? And what becomes of the people who need assistance? I do not hear sirens or ambulances, only screams and wailing.

I feel barely alive, like a cloth wrung out and twisted so many times it is bone dry.

All around me, the religious Jews are praying with gratitude, believing their prayers have been answered. But I think differently. Our group of hostages has been spared, but not our neighbors, who have probably also been praying—to a different god. And there is no guarantee we will be so fortunate the next time. The smell of burning flesh from the nearby house is nauseating and brings me back to our reality. Our hope for survival. We rise slowly from the floor and stagger back to our rooms.

The following day, we hear a heavy tank rolling up our street, and again, shelling is close. We rush to the hallway. Our guard, Mohammed, has been forewarned by other PFLP members that the Jordanian army is close by; he and another guard stand inside the door with a hand grenade and guns to protect us. He instructs us to stay away from the windows so we will not be discovered. The Jordanian soldiers are probably unaware of where we are being held, and the PFLP needs to protect us however they can from being accidently killed or, I suppose, rescued.

After the Jordanian army tank has left our street, Mohammed is relieved and talks to Rachel. "They came so close to this apartment. They were within twenty-five feet of our building."

It doesn't fully occur to us until later that if we had just run out the door or screamed, maybe the Jordanian army could have saved us. But in those tense moments, we didn't understand enough of the dynamics. And we are accustomed to obeying the Palestinians' orders.

When the shooting and bombing redirect to another part of Amman, we have a brief reprieve. I lie on my mat, close my eyes, and hum the Beatles' "Here Comes the Sun" and "We all Live in a Yellow Submarine." I sing a bit aloud and Shoshana and Rachel sometimes join. I imagine I'm back at college, walking to classes with friends or playing with my friend Mark's Scottish terrier at the park, or I float weightlessly in the healing mineral waters of the Dead Sea. My fantasy travels take me to safer, happier places.

We each have our own distractions.

Rachel and Shoshana fantasize they'll be back home for the next Sabbath dinner, describing how their favorite foods, lovingly prepared by their mothers, will await them. David and Abe, both religious college students, talk about being home for Rosh Hashanah, which is fast approaching. Bob and Ben play card games. Mike and I continue to play Scrabble frequently, amusing one another with made-up words.

The religious men find solace in prayer. A few have managed to hang on to their prayer books. Others recite verses from memory in hushed whispers throughout the day. At prescribed times, they all rise and pray, bodies swaying. One day, I ask Abe why Jews pray that way. I've seen it many times but never thought to ask. He explains when a person prays, the light of his or her soul is kindled; swaying resembles the flame of a candle. It also helps deepen concentration.

In contrast, one of the TWA crew members is an outspoken atheist and apparently offended by these pious displays of religion. He entertains himself by provoking several observant college students, questioning them about their beliefs and practices, the apparent futility of their devotion, and their unwillingness to eat nonkosher food. I try not to listen. The tension is bad enough without this bickering.

Seated cross-legged on a mat near me is a quiet guy named Daniel, who has further withdrawn since the war began. For what seems like hours, he plays an imaginary drum, hands moving across an invisible set, head bobbing in rhythm with imagined sounds. We don't know how to reach the world into which he has retreated. Sometimes when we talk to him, he doesn't respond.

Daniel's behavior troubles me because it's familiar; My older brother, Joel, lives in his own world, too. But it wasn't until my sister was in college that any of us learned what was wrong with him. Her psychology professor had lectured about schizophrenia, mentioning symptoms like talking with people who weren't there and hearing voices. Armed with this knowledge, my sister urged our parents to take Joel to a psychiatrist who could diagnose him and provide appropriate treatment. They refused, still hoping he would "grow out of the phase he was in." It wasn't until he was in his twenties that he finally started treatment. He remains a disturbed man. Here in captivity, I don't know what has caused Daniel's withdrawal—it could be our situation—but it makes me uncomfortable to be around him.

There's a general sense among us that we must try to keep up group morale, because our emotions are contagious. If one person breaks, we could all be at risk. It's a small space for so many people, some of whom I would not have chosen to spend a few hours with, let alone a few weeks. We all need to contain ourselves, not fall apart.

We are a line of dominoes, balancing tentatively on edge, leaning on each other for support. One flick of a finger would be enough for the whole row of us to fall, toppling in quick succession.

When there are no imminent attacks nearby, Mohammed and other guards try to bring food and water. Our meals are now meager portions of pita bread, sardines, and orange jam, and I eat slowly to make them last. Vegetables and fruits are scarce in the city, but they manage to bring us six lemons, which we cut and divide among the thirty-two of us. I savor the sour taste. We ration our water supply carefully, now just a small cup a day.

A few of the kosher hostages are now eating with the rest of us, having realized they need food to maintain their strength. But others still do not allow themselves to eat the tinned food as the jam and sardines do not have a required "OU," indicating that they have been prepared in accord with kosher regulations. It's distressing to see them exist on nothing but bread and limited water. But the Palestinians respect their dietary restrictions and try to bring additional simple provisions of bread and rice so they will not go hungry. We appreciate Mohammed's attempts to provide for them, despite the grim conditions.

The fighting stops at night or at least is not as loud, reducing our anxiety and making it possible to sleep.

We can't risk lighting candles inside the front room at night, because if seen from outside it could invite a volley of shots or grenades. In the kitchen, it is relatively safe to light a makeshift oil lamp fashioned out of empty sardine cans and a bit of oil; wicks are thin strips of cloth cut from a burlap bag. The dim, flickering light draws us together to talk, laugh, and smoke.

We learn from a radio broadcast that, so far, the civil war has destroyed hundreds of houses in Amman and damaged thousands more. Civilians fear going outside because they may be shot. Hundreds of wounded people lie in the streets, but it is impossible for either the Jordanian Red Crescent or the International Red Cross to provide medical care as snipers roam the area. Hospitals overflow with the wounded. Describing the devastation as "worse than a powerful earthquake," the Jordanian government has requested urgent medical aid from other countries.

At the end of the broadcast, the sound crackles and becomes faint. The radio batteries have died; our sources of news now will be solely what we can see out the window when we dare to look and what our guards choose to share with us, if anything.

When our sardine-can lamps burn out, we return to our thin mattresses. I'm usually a good sleeper—with the exception of nights spent sitting up on the plane. I'm more fortunate than other hostages who toss and turn, and others who need to use the bathroom at night, who stumble in the darkness over the rest of us to find their way. The mornings are filled with the grumbling of those whom sleep has eluded. Our faces show the accumulating exhaustion that makes keeping our spirits up more and more challenging.

Some of us resort to gallows humor. Our favorite topic is imagining in exquisite detail our magnificent funeral. We envision our bodies, flown home on a United States Air Force plane from Jordan, laid in military caskets as soon as we are back on American soil. We are driven down Pennsylvania Avenue on caissons. Each of the thirty-two caskets is wrapped in an American flag that has flown over the White House. As per tradition, the blue part of the flag is placed at the head of the coffin. Each casket is carried in a separate carriage, creating a long procession. Wreaths of fragrant white flowers, flown in from all over the country, are overflowing on each horse-drawn carriage. Six large black horses pull each caisson; in all, our procession includes 192 horses. Each caisson is driven by a high-ranking military officer in full dress uniform. All government offices in Washington DC are closed in honor of our funeral, and flags are required to fly at half-mast.

As each new detail is offered up, we laugh, embellishing or rejecting each other's ideas.

"I'm imagining this is something like the Macy's Thanksgiving Day parade," I say. "Lots of people out, crowding the streets."

Bob disagrees. "No! That makes me think of decorated floats and high school marching bands. This is a serious occasion, and the circumstances of our deaths demand a solemn procession."

We agree that the streets will be lined with mournful, handkerchief-gripping men, women, and children, who never knew us but ardently wish they had. We are revered as heroes, like those who have been awarded purple hearts or medals of honor. Mourners are dressed in black to show respect, and hundreds of soldiers in full regalia, carrying rifles, march by the White House, where President Nixon weeps uncontrollably, realizing too late he could have intervened and saved us. By his side, Henry Kissinger also weeps tears of regret.

I insist the procession also travel down the street where I lived in Washington. My roommate, Karen, my downstairs neighbors, Neil and Annie, all my college friends, even my black cat, Krishna, will all stand and sob as my casket rolls by.

Thinking up new details is a regular pastime. Each telling and retelling of the tale of our deaths and funeral procession occasions gales of laughter. Just like at home, laughter is a safe way of communicating emotion without addressing fears that lie beneath the surface, where our most pressing questions remain unanswered: Does the U.S. government know where we're being held, and what—if anything—are they doing to get us home? If negotiations with the PFLP are taking place, why is it taking so long? How is the civil war affecting prospects of our release? We haven't seen a newspaper for days. I wonder if the released European hostages have been able to contact my parents.

When the hijackings first occurred, we were all over the TV news and newspaper headlines. Journalists took photographs and pilots gave interviews. But media attention was short-lived and now, three weeks later, we believe our hostage story might be insignificant on the global stage, worthy of only a paragraph in the back section of the newspaper.

Later, after my return home, I learned that our fears were well founded. An article in the *New York Times* noted, "Virtually forgotten in the civil war crisis were the airline hostages held in guerrilla territory in and around Amman, in the direct path of military occupation."

Other articles reported that the U.S. government believed the American hostages were still being held in Jordan, but that we had been moved outside of Amman. The civil war made it difficult—if not impossible—for them to contact Palestinian leaders to determine our location and negotiate for our release.

One *New York Times* article quoted a PFLP spokesperson who announced that the shelling in Amman "made no difference for the release of the hostages" and confirmed "it is very dangerous for them." Of the circumstances of our captivity, he said, "They are on the same level as our people; we cannot give them better shelter than the shelter we give ourselves."

The Palestinian Red Crescent confirmed hundreds of wounded were dying in the streets of Amman for lack of medical attention and called for medical supplies and first aid teams. There were already between 5,000 and 10,000 wounded and dead in the city, and thousands more were said to have been killed in the refugee camps, a prime target of the Jordanian army.

Despite the rising number of casualties, the guerrillas still hoped to topple King Hussein's government and replace it with a government that would focus on restoring ancestral lands to Palestinians. The PFLP would not be satisfied with "overtaking Jordan and calling it Palestine." I was surprised to learn that the number of Palestinians living in Jordan had come to comprise between 50 and 60 percent of the country's population, a force to be reckoned with.

Our hijacking was intertwined with the larger political struggle occurring in the Middle East. President Nasser of Egypt, President Nimeiry of Sudan, and Libyan leader Qaddafi had sent a joint message to Jordan to halt the civil war, which they characterized as a tragedy. Baghdad radio charged that the United States was poised to invade the Middle East under the pretext of saving the hostages.

Newspapers reported there was no information about our fate. Seven days after the planes were blown up, the *New York Times* quoted the U.S. secretary of defense, "We feel all American hostages held in Jordan are still alive," although there was no mention of what had led them to that conclusion. They editorialized that Western military intervention could no longer save us; the situation was too complicated, delicate, and dangerous. Op-eds advocated for intensified negotiations among the nations involved to "save the citizens who are victims of this savage reversion to medieval barbarism."

In the apartment in Amman, we frequently ask our guards when we are going home, but we receive no information. The Palestinians are busy with the civil war, trying to stay alive themselves. Laila and Nadia have not returned since those early visits with our group of women, and I wonder if they are fighting on the streets or have died in battle. I already doubt I'll ever find out what's happened to them.

About eight days into the war, Mohammed tells Rachel the PFLP are considering letting half of us go, although he does not offer details about who that will include. This rumor throws us into a panic, particularly we four young women, who seem to be left behind every time we are sorted into groups. This would be the grand finale: If just a small group of us remain hostage, our captors could easily move us around the country. Then, it would be even more difficult to find us. Assuming anyone is looking.

We beg to send a letter or telegram to the International Red Cross, so we can remind them there are thirty-two Americans in grave danger in Amman. But Mohammed shakes his head: There is no one to carry a message for us and no way to send it. Amman is shuttered. Any Palestinians caught in the street will be shot dead.

The next day, Mohammed leaves to fetch us water. He doesn't return. We wonder if maybe he's gone home to care for his wife and children. Another Palestinian, whom we have not seen before, takes his place by the front door, keeping a watch on what is going on outside our apartment.

In Arabic, Rachel inquires, "Where's Mohammed? We haven't seen him today."

The new guard is distraught. "He was walking up the hill with the water jugs when a bomb exploded near him."

A wave of choking sadness rises inside me. I gasp.

Mohammed was trying to care for us when he died. I imagine his family gathered in their small house, crying, wailing, grieving for the loss of their father and husband. It has never been clearer to me how fragile life is, how quickly we can be extinguished, how close we are to death every moment of these long days.

DAYS 18–20

THE FINAL DAYS

Without a radio, we rely on Rachel to ask the guards about the war. She learns there is continued heavy fighting across Jordan and casualties of both civilians and Palestinian militants are rising. Negotiations for a ceasefire are underway but do not seem promising. Diplomats from the Jordanian government and the Palestinian side have traveled to Cairo to work out a deal but have returned unsuccessful.

Water service has been restored to some parts of Amman, but we remain without a trickle. It's been six days since I've brushed my teeth, and the sour taste in my mouth is disgusting. I should be used to this by now.

One evening we are gathering in the kitchen when mortar shells explode outside within twenty feet of where we sit. The floor shakes. The explosions make my ears ring, and the acrid odor makes me dizzy and nauseated. We shudder to think what could have been. We blow out our sardine-can lamp, scurry back to our rooms, and try to sleep.

The next day, several guerrillas rush into our apartment. They are talking fast, gesturing with their hands. They seem frantic.

"You are no longer safe here," one man says. "You could be blown up! You must write to your president, to the Red Cross, to anybody! The PFLP cannot protect you anymore. We'll send telegrams!"

Tension grips my neck and shoulders; sweat gathers on my brow. I've never seen these guerrillas like this; they seem genuinely panicked. I don't understand what's going on or what's changed. Why can't they protect us anymore—if they ever really could in the first place? Is the Jordanian army targeting this part of town? Is the PFLP summoning all its soldiers to come fight them?

A guerrilla tells us we need to write a short message that can be sent as telegrams to world leaders. He gives us paper and a pen. We write: "The situation here is very dangerous. We are in the midst of a violent war. The PFLP are doing their best to protect us but we may be killed at any moment. Please arrange for our immediate release." We address our letters to President Nixon, Golda Meir, the Red Cross, even the pope. We're desperate to get the word out.

The guerrillas ask Captain Woods and other crew to join them outside to witness the devastation on the streets.

When they return, the unsettled look on our pilot's usually stoic face says more than his words. "It was awful," he says. "Demolished buildings, rubble everywhere, dead bodies. There's no one alive outside. I wonder if they've all run away somewhere, hiding until the shelling stops. We're lucky we've survived this long. The PFLP are absolutely right—we're not safe here. They thought we were safe because this building backs up to a hill, but now that houses close to us have been blown up, they know ours could be, too. There's no telling what can happen."

My heart beats hard against my ribs.

"We've written the telegrams. How can we speed up our release? How about we just walk out of here now?" Ben says.

"That's not a good idea," Captain Woods replies, his voice solemn. "Too dangerous. Be patient. They're negotiating for our release."

In preparation, we change into our own clothes. Feeling exposed, back in my minidress, I pull on my pajama pants to cover my legs. It's a bizarre, mismatched outfit, but I don't want to call the wrong kind of attention to myself.

Fighting continues, but at a distance. In the early afternoon, a guard informs us that a ceasefire agreement has been reached. While this seems exciting news, I don't trust it, knowing our situation can change in a moment. How will we ever get out of here, and where will we go when we finally do?

The next day, the guerrillas arrive at our apartment and ask Captain Woods to accompany them to the Egyptian embassy to arrange for our release. We're all on edge, anxious to finally leave.

"It will be dangerous to find our way by foot," they warn him, "and you may not be able to come back here."

Still, the captain agrees to go. What other hope do we have? We worry for their safety, but there is nothing we can do but wait.

We're used to waiting by now—but this time, it doesn't last long. Within hours, an unfamiliar PFLP member and a man from the Egyptian embassy rush into the apartment and announce, *"You're free. Gather your things.*

Red Cross buses will meet you. Hold up something white to show you are coming in peace."

We are all elated and jump up, ready to leave immediately. While waiting for them to return, we've put all our shoes by the front door, so our departure will be easy. I hug Rachel, Shoshana, and Susan. But our hopes have been shattered many times before, so all we can do is breathe a sigh of relief even if many of us—including me—are riddled with doubts about whether we are really going home, As we file out of the apartment for the first time in thirteen days, we must remain steely, ready to face whatever we find on the streets.

We gather up the few things we have. I don't have anything white, but Rachel has a white handkerchief, so I walk next to her. Shoshana has one, too, so Susan will be by her side. A few men clutch white undershirts, ready to wave them high as we step out of the building onto the street for the first time. The observant Jews, who are never permitted to carry anything on the Sabbath, give what few belongings they have to others.

Outside, I shield my eyes from the late afternoon sunlight. We've been told the fighting devastated the area, but nothing could prepare us for seeing it firsthand. The putrid smell of smoldering flesh fills the air.

My eyes fall on a child's bicycle, charred and twisted in the sand. Nearby, a small leg, partly buried under the ash. I can hardly bear to look yet I cannot turn away.

Weak from dehydration and inadequate food, we walk unsteadily down the hill. Some of us have not walked more than a few steps outside since the hijacking. Rachel and I link arms for support, and Shoshana and Susan do the same. Two of the young religious men walk beside Rabbi and Mrs. Greenberg, offering support. I am far too nervous and shaky to feel relief at being outside, even with the promise of freedom.

As we reach the bottom of the hill, an emaciated young mother in a green robe approaches us, a crying infant in her arms. The tiny baby, wrapped in tattered cloth, appears to be two or three months old. The woman thrusts the bundle toward Rachel and me. Tears running down her cheeks, she speaks to us in Arabic.

"What did she say?" I ask. Though her gestures are unmistakable, I need confirmation.

Rachel translates in a horrified monotone. "Please, take my son. He will have a better life in your country than here. He will be safe with you."

Rachel and I gaze at the woman's tragic face. "No, no, we can't," Rachel says in Arabic. She moves to thrust the baby into our arms, and instinctively we put up our hands to block her. I feel sad for her—and for her infant—but am clear I am in no position to help them.

The young mother desperately runs to Shoshana and Susan and holds her baby out to them. They shake their heads vehemently and with sorrow, affirming they do not want her infant. The four of us quicken our pace, avoiding the mother's gaze, hoping we will find the Red Cross bus waiting close by before more survivors find us.

The Egyptian official is walking at the front of our group, waving a white flag. He seems to be in charge, leading us to meet the buses, but after some walking, we still haven't found them. Is there really a set location where we are supposed to find the Red Cross? Were they intercepted by gunfire or unable to enter the roads blocked by tanks?

Our large, conspicuously foreign group wanders the streets for a long hour surrounded by demolished buildings and storefronts with blown-out windows. Broken glass is strewn on the road. Abandoned cars rest in the middle of the street. In the distance, the threat of mortar fire and black smoke.

Bands of adolescent boys—young fedayeen—probably not more than fourteen or fifteen years old, roam the empty streets with guns, ready to shoot without provocation. I wonder if it's because they have seen so much killing. Maybe they need to feel powerful.

Whatever the reason, the house we have just left because it was too dangerous now seems safer than these streets.

When our group of girls falls a short distance behind the men, we are approached by another group of militants; they look nine or ten years old. One boy's cheeks are still round with baby fat. Another holds his gun awkwardly, as if he hasn't held one before. When they motion us to stand in front of a nearby building, we obey. Our guide witnesses the interaction and orders them to leave us alone. They comply, apparently accustomed to following adults' instructions.

By now, I doubt the Red Cross will ever be able to find us. We duck into a deserted Camel cigarette factory and sit on the loading dock, where we can see the street and watch for the buses. Soon, another band of young men with guns find us.

"These are the PFLP hostages. Leave them alone!" the Egyptian shouts angrily. "They are being freed and Red Cross buses are looking for them. Protect them from others who might want to harm them."

Rather than shoot us, which I suspect was their intention, they sit watch for other militants. Another small miracle.

The cigarette factory is not operating, because of the war, but it has a toilet with a small sink with running water. We wash our faces and hands for the first time in countless days and drink the metallic-tasting water from the faucet, able at last to quench our throats and dehydrated bodies. Some men smoke cigarettes and celebratory cigars they found in a box.

I am not ready to celebrate. Despite having been told we are free, we still sit and wait for two hours, mostly in silence. There is so much to worry about, even now. Maybe even more than before. What if the Red Cross doesn't show up? Or if another band of wandering militants appear, shoot our new "guards," and take us hostage? I can't control these dark thoughts that shoot like piercing arrows into my troubled head.

It's dusk when Red Cross vans finally arrive. A man introduces himself as a representative of the group and informs us we will be driven to the Muashir hospital in Amman, where we will spend the night. He explains the long wait: The convoy was stopped several times and refused passage through the streets. As we leave the building, machine gun fire suddenly erupts in our direction. We flatten ourselves against the outside structure of the building, holding our breath, praying we can avoid the bullets. After a few minutes, we sprint into the four vans; we four women squeeze into a row. When we are settled, the vans speed off to the hospital.

I imagined the moment of freedom to be one of great excitement and happiness. But fear clings, its tentacles having reached deep inside me over the last three weeks.

When we reach the outskirts of the city, the Red Cross representative says, "We'll be crossing a no man's land soon. The next few miles are a dangerous stretch of road planted with land mines and snipers."

My heart races. Not again. Every moment is packed with its own dangers, sometimes seen, sometimes hidden. Rachel, Shoshana, Susan, and I huddle close to one another. An eerie silence has descended on our van.

For the first mile, the "no man's land" is a flat stretch, devoid of trees and shrubs, reminiscent of the desert surrounding the planes. Farther along, there are mounds of sand and scrubby bushes where snipers may be lying in wait, perched to ambush our bus. There is no way to know if land mines have been planted along the dusty unpaved road. Maybe a band of guerrillas will appear in Land Rovers full of guns and grenades. They could kill us in minutes, or we could be taken hostage again by another Palestinian terrorist group.

Our only defense is to crouch away from the windows. I'm bent over in my seat, once again hoping, praying, we'll get through this final stretch without incident. We are so close to freedom and, again, it feels so far away.

Thankfully, we arrive at the hospital without incident, and hospital staff greet us warmly. They bring us to a large room where orange juice and cheese sandwiches await, our first food of the day. The Egyptian man who guided us through the streets is no longer with us, and we are now in the hands of hospital workers.

I feel numb, worried about what will come next. We are not out of the country yet and don't know when we will leave. After the meal, our group is taken to an adjacent building where we will spend the night. Rachel, Shoshana, Susan, and I are given a small room with four narrow cots. The room has no windows; a single light bulb dangles from the ceiling. The bathroom has a small sink and a squat toilet, and only a dribble of running water. Still, we're grateful to have a separate space, away from the smell and sounds of the hospital.

As I try to sleep, I wonder if this is the freedom we've been expecting. It doesn't feel that way. We're in limbo, uncertain where we'll be going next. Though we were told we are headed home, no one has told us how we are going to get there.

None of us has a passport.

In the morning, two nurses knock on our door and instruct us to follow them to the hospital's emergency department. The halls reek of the stench of unwashed bodies and the smell of decay.

Patients wounded in the fighting, some on gurneys, others on the floor, overflow in the narrow space. Many do not have sheets under them. With health-care workers stretched to their limit, some of the wounded moan loudly.

The white linoleum floor is stained with blood.

We move from the open hallways to the crowded children's ward. The nurses lift the sheets from several of the most critically wounded children, revealing horrendous injuries.

Some have lost a hand, others a leg. Children have their heads swathed in bandages. Some are awake and stare wide-eyed at us. They are young, fragile, and maimed for life.

It is heart-rending to see these mutilated children and the other casualties of war. Not only are they physically and psychologically scarred, but who knows if their parents or siblings are still alive? Without medical supplies and drugs to treat them, their outlook is bleak. What will life offer a legless child living in a refugee camp? I need to cry but hold my tears. One girl's tears seem a paltry response to the magnitude of suffering.

One of the nurses speaks to us in Arabic. "This is what King Hussein and his army have done to our Palestinian children. The king had his soldiers harm children so they could never become soldiers and fight against him. He is angry because of the destruction and devastation in Amman and all over his country. Many Jordanian soldiers and civilians have burned to death during this war. It is forbidden for Muslims to die by burning. But you Americans are responsible too—your government supports Israel and have forced us Palestinians to be refugees here."

Rachel translates, though it is hard for me to concentrate on what she is saying and difficult to understand the politics behind these violent assaults on children. I feel sick. My head throbs. I'm teetering at my edge, weary and unable to withstand the pain and suffering that surround us. I stand silently, trying to suppress my emotions and thoughts.

The nurse offers her parting words in English: "Remember these children always."

PART 3

DAYS 21–22

RELEASE

At 6:00 the next morning, we reunite with the other hostages for a small breakfast. Shortly afterward, we are driven by bus to the Amman airport, where there's a Red Cross DC-6 plane waiting for us on the runway.

I'm nervous about getting on another plane. Rachel flat-out refuses to get on, terrified that Palestinian militants would come aboard and drag her off. One of the TWA crew somehow coaxes her to come onboard. Shoshana and I, also feeling nervous about getting on, clasp hands with Rachel and walk up the stairs into the plane. She sits in the back with a friendly crew member. I take a seat next to Bob.

"Hey, it's like old times, right? We started together and here we are again, back on a plane. Did you hear we're going to Beirut—not Cyprus, where all the other hostages were taken?" This information was circulating minutes ago as we waited on the runway to board the plane.

Bob sighs. "I heard that too, but I sure hope it's not true. Maybe the pilot will let us know once we're in the air."

Sure enough, like always, Bob was right. A few moments after takeoff from the smoldering ruins of Amman, the pilot announces that we are headed to Nicosia, Cyprus. We learn from a crew member that the original plan was to fly to Beirut, but the pilot called in a medical emergency that required us to land in Nicosia. I don't understand the politics of it—no one has an emergency that I know of—but I am happy to learn we are finally headed to a friendly country.

"We're on our way home, Bob!" I exclaim, finally willing to let out my excitement. "It only took us twenty-one days!"

We high five each other, grinning, acknowledging that we are finally free.

I'm ready to regain agency, to take over my own life. Maybe soon.

Our pilot announces that flight time is approximately one hour. We aren't told how long we will stay in Nicosia or how we'll enter the country without passports or identification. I'm tired of worrying. The coolness of the air conditioning helps me nap. I awake with a nudge from Bob. "We're here. It's freedom time!" he says, his face lighting up in a smile of delight and relief.

As I wait to disembark, I hug Rachel, Shoshana, Susan, and Mike. The moment we've been waiting for, praying for—is finally here.

All thirty-two of us released captives, rumpled and confused at what happens next, trudge to the Nicosia International Airport transit lounge, where reporters and photographers press around us. Despite our belief that the world had forgotten us, it turns out we're big news—at least now that we've been recovered safely. I need to shift gears from hostage to celebrity.

An American NBC reporter bombards Rachel and me with questions: "How were you treated? Do you know why they kept you? Did they threaten to kill you? Did you think you'd get out alive? How did you get free?"

I give short answers, but Rachel is silent. Maybe she's had enough of her role as translator and spokesperson. Now it's my turn.

Finally, our group is driven to the Cyprus Hilton, where we are given keys to our own rooms for the night. TWA is covering the cost of the hotel, meals, clothes, toiletries, and phone calls. In the hotel boutique, I find a dizzying array of costly Western clothes; I choose a blue and white blouse, black cotton pants, panties, and a bra. I've gone down three sizes, which hardly seems possible—I wonder if European sizing is different. I also get a toothbrush, toothpaste, a hairbrush, and Chapstick.

Alone in the elevator, I'm jumpy, half expecting a Palestinian guerrilla or sympathizer to appear and drag me back into captivity. I lock my door, undress, and toss my filthy clothes on the floor. The silence is unsettling after three weeks in the close and constant company of others.

After weeks of daydreams about washing off dust and dirt in a proper shower, I take the longest, hottest shower I've ever taken, soaping and rinsing, soaping and rinsing, luxuriating in the floral aroma of the shampoo and conditioner. The murky water washes away layers of sand; I hope fear will wash down the drain with the grime.

Naked before a full-length mirror, I hardly recognize the girl who stares back at me. Her cheeks are sunken, her eyes dull and lifeless. She's thinner than she's ever been. She can see the contour of her ribs. Someone

I Was a Hijack Hostage

A Freed Mother's Own Story • Starts Today on Page 41

WEATHER
Partly sunny and cool, mid 60s
Tonight: Clear and cool, mid 40s
Tomorrow: Sunny, continued cool, 60s
Fair and milder Wed.

New York Post

FOUNDED 1801, THE OLDEST CONTINUOUSLY PUBLISHED DAILY IN THE UNITED STATES.

NEW YORK, MONDAY, SEPTEMBER 28, 1970
© 1970 New York Post Corporation
15 Cents

LATE CITY
OVER THE COUNTER

Arab Treaty Puts the Heat Back on Israel

Associated Press Cablephoto

PRESIDENT NIXON chats with Italian President Giuseppe Saragat after the two exchanged official greetings at the Presidential Palace in Rome. Tonight Nixon visits the 6th Fleet, on duty in the Mediterranean. Page 4.

Combined Cable Dispatches

The pressure was back on Israel today with the signing of an Arab agreement ending the Jordanian civil war.

Lebanon, which has suffered heavily from Israeli retaliatory strikes because of guerrilla attacks made from behind its borders, guarded against a renewal of such terrorist raids.

Observers at Tiberias, Israel, reported that Lebanese troops were out in force along their common border, apparently in anticipation of increased guerrilla activity.

Since the outbreak of the civil war on Sept. 17, Israel has been spared the usual guerrilla attacks from Jordan and Lebanon. And there has been no activity on the Suez front because of the 90-day ceasefire in effect there.

The Jordanian peace agreement, signed yesterday in Cairo by King Hussein of Jordan, Palestinian commando leader Yasir Arafat and eight Arab nations, set up a three-man committee to insure that its provisions are carried out and to report any violations to the co-signing states.

Foremost among the agreement's 14 points is that Hussein's army and the Palestinian forces will withdraw from Amman, almost destroyed by 10 days of fighting. The soldiers were to return to their normal barracks and the guerrillas to positions "best suited to their activities" in the "liberation battle against Israel"—presumably the Israel-Jordan ceasefire line along the Jordan River.

The pact prohibits "all propaganda campaigns"

Continued on Page 5

The Captives: No Time for Tears

By Perry Young
N. Y. Post Correspondent

NICOSIA, Cyprus—It was the happiest group involved in the Middle East crisis.

They were laughing and drinking and singing the songs they sang to pass the time during their incredible ordeal as hostages of the Popular Front for the Liberation of Palestine.

"Can you believe it, we didn't even know each other before all this?" said Benny Feinstein, 38, of Whitestone, Queens, as we sat down at a boisterous dinner party in the Hilton Hotel here where the hostages were flown yesterday after three weeks of captivity in Jordan.

"In real life we'd try to kill each other getting on the subway but nine days with 32 people in two rooms with no bathroom or water can really do it," said Feinstein.

[Twenty-eight of the 32 hostages left for New York today on a TWA jetliner. Their plane touched down in Rome and President Nixon, on a state visit there, made an unscheduled trip to the airport to greet them.

[There was no explanation as to why four of the former captives remained in Cyprus.

[Six other hostages remained in Amman, but diplomatic sources said they too had been freed, and were being taken care of by the Egyptian embassy, acting as a go-between for the International Red Cross.]

They completely overwhelmed everybody in the hotel with their lively spirit and hilarity. An elderly British couple stood in genuine awe, explaining, "You know, the whole world has worried and worried about these people and we just can't believe they are safe and alive and happy now."

"The team" of younger hostages seemed to have taken over the problem of morale right from the beginning of the hijackings. Sarah Malka, 20, of North Bergen, N. J., was the sardine and canned beans chief and Feinstein made the tea "which we

Continued on Page 58

MIRIAM BEEBER

SARAH MALKA

ON THE INSIDE

HELP WANTED: The Democrats need a "boss." Page 2.

THE CABBIES' day of mourning. Page 3.

HARRIS POLL: Muskie and Nixon neck and neck. Page 4.

THE METS: Rest In Peace. Back Page.

FIG. 11. Upon arriving in Nicosia, Cyprus, Mimi Nichter was overwhelmed by media anxious to hear of her hostage experience. Author's collection.

might describe her as lanky, not a word that would have been a match for her before-body. She's a shadow of the energetic girl who boarded the plane in Tel Aviv. Weariness has crept into her bones and sapped her body of its youthful energy.

I collapse on the bed in a cozy hotel bathrobe, and my long, wet hair dries in a fluffy towel. I marvel at the clean, air-conditioned room, the

FIG. 12. Mimi Nichter (*center*) and two other women hostages in Nicosia, Cyprus, one day after their release. AP photo.

FIG. 13. Mimi Nichter in Nicosia, Cyprus. From Reuters archives video, "Italy: President Nixon Makes Surprise Visit to Rome Airport to Meet Released Hijack Hostages" (1970).

bed with its thick mattress and cotton mustard-colored bedspread, and the small refrigerator that contains bottles of regular and bubbly water, Coca-Cola, Dr Pepper, Snickers bars, and M&Ms. Was it just yesterday that I was in Jordan among the wounded and maimed children? And the day before amid bombs and the threat of imminent death? I'm overwhelmed by this world I've reentered, a world awash with personal choice. I've traveled from a place of extreme thirst to a collection of cold water and sodas at my fingertips, from a lack of food to a fridge filled with chocolate candies. From hardship to bounty.

There's a yellow princess phone on the nightstand with instructions for making an international call. I've called home just a few times before from a foreign country. But this time is different. When I was living in London, I called my parents out of obligation, to fill them in on my schooling and life abroad. But now I'm calling to reassure them I'm okay, that I've made it out alive, to tell them how happy I'll be to see them.

Without a thought to the time in New York, I dial the "0" to connect to the overseas operator.

"How can I help you?" the operator asks, her voice distant and crackling.

"I want to make a call to the United States. The phone number is 212-377-4391."

"What is the name of the party you're calling?" she asks.

"I'm calling for Mrs. Essy Beeber," I say, picturing the black rotary-dial phone on a wooden table, amid piles of *Life* magazine and days-old *New York Times*, beside the sofa. How close I am to being home, and yet how far away I feel. I hear clicking, then the distant, familiar ring of the phone and, at last, my mother's faint hello over the staticky line.

"Mom, it's me," I say, my voice shaky. "We got released yesterday. We flew from Amman to Cyprus this morning. I'm at the Hilton. Don't worry, I'm still in one piece, I'm safe." I cry softly, not wanting to upset her. "I'll be home tomorrow!"

"I'm so happy to finally hear your voice," she says, her words overflowing with relief and joy. I imagine her clutching her blue, embroidered handkerchief, blotting tears from her powdered cheeks. "We've been so worried! We just got a telegram from the State Department saying all thirty-two hostages have been flown out of Amman. TWA called too, to let us know you're on your way home. I've been waiting by the phone, knowing you'd be calling."

She tells me that since the hijacking she has been in frequent contact with the State Department and was planning a trip to Washington in a few days with other hostage families to fight for our release. How naive I've been to think they didn't know where I was. My father must be in Philadelphia at work, because he doesn't get on the phone. That is what I'd expect; Mother is there sometimes, Dad hardly ever. Still, the call is a comfort and afterward I can finally rest.

I fall into my first deep sleep in weeks, enjoying the crispness of the white sheets, the cleanliness of my body, and the coolness of the room. I awake with a phone call from Shoshana, who tells me there's a plan for all of us to meet for dinner in the hotel restaurant. Most of our group of ex-hostages join us. I take a seat next to Mike, and we immediately start to joke.

"I'd probably like one of everything," Mike says, his eyes sparkling. I notice he's shaved and washed his hair.

"Sure, you're a hungry guy. Go for it! But first, shouldn't we start with celebratory drinks?" I suggest.

I order a Vodka Collins and Mike has a beer. When the drinks arrive at the table, Ben stands and raises his whiskey. "To all of us, we're finally free and heading home tomorrow! Mazel Tov!"

We continue to drink alcohol and feast. After having so little food for the past few weeks, I'm thrilled with the choices on the menu. I settle on basic American fare: a hamburger, french fries, and a Coke, which I gobble down.

As we sit around the table, I look at the others and appreciate the bond that has formed among us, the uncomplicated friendships we all forged for survival. We needed each other during those long, dark days. And now, after all we've gone through together, we are about to move on to our "real" lives.

The alcohol has made me drowsy, and I return to my room and my nice soft bed.

I rise early and revel in another hot shower. Drying off, I look out the window at the swimming pool, surrounded by bright green grass and trees full of lovely purple flowers, a visual treat after weeks in the desert.

I realize that soon—even now—I can walk out the door and appreciate the outdoors whenever I want.

By the time room service arrives with my breakfast, I'm dressed in my new clothes. The smell of the food is a delight: I enjoy my first cup of hot coffee in weeks, pancakes covered in maple syrup, and fresh fruit. Miraculously, I find the small Jewish star on a gold chain in the pocket of my minidress, the necklace I took off after we landed in Jordan. I put it on, a symbolic statement to myself that I no longer need to fear being Jewish.

At 9:00 a.m., twenty-six of us former hostages, all American, gather in the Hilton lobby and board a bus for the airport, where a TWA charter flight to New York awaits us. We are the only passengers aboard, with a full crew. The other six ex-hostages left earlier and are flying on a Lear jet with a CBS reporter who wants an exclusive interview with them. I have no idea who is participating—I think it's one or two of the crew and some others. I don't know why the others were selected. The other women and Mike and Bob are still with me on our TWA plane. I'm thankful I wasn't selected. We've got a huge plane for our small group and we're all happy. I sit next to Mike, knowing that we'll have a few good laughs, hopefully more raucous than ever. After takeoff, we learn our plane will make a short refueling stop in Rome.

During the descent into Rome's airport, the captain announces that President Nixon, who is visiting the pope in Italy, will be meeting us there. Everyone seems excited by this announcement, except me. Where were the president and his administration when we needed them? Did they do anything to promote our release? I resent being used as a photo opportunity to bolster Nixon's image. Several of our group believe that our release from Amman owed little to American diplomacy or intervention. We had become a liability for the PFLP, so they chose to release us. If we had been killed in the civil war, the hijackings and subsequent detention of Americans would have been in vain.

Most of the hostages eagerly shake Nixon's hand, pose for photos, and request the president's autograph. He asks each of them where they are from and engages in a short conversation. Shoshana, however, challenges the president with sarcasm, "We've been worried about you. We haven't heard from you in three weeks."

I remain on the airplane steps and let out a few loud yippees. This was a popular strategy my friends and I used at political rallies in Washington when we protested the war in Vietnam. "Yipping" was a tactic, along with street theater, used by the counterculture Youth International Party to disrupt political events. I didn't plan to do it at this airport, but seeing the other hostages fawn over Nixon reminds me of my political beliefs. The college student who protested U.S. imperialist actions around the world reemerges. My subversive behavior is quickly extinguished by a TWA crew member who directs me back inside the plane and tells me to be quiet. I comply with his request; what I've been doing is probably inappropriate in this moment. But it feels good to be back in a world where I can express myself freely without fear of someone holding a gun to my head. Before long, Nixon is back on Air Force One and we are on our way to New York. Nobody asks me why I yipped or if yipping has a special meaning.

The rest of the flight home is restful as we spread out on our own seats. I watch part of a movie then decide to spend the remaining time visiting with friends—sharing our excitement about going home, and saying my final goodbyes to the other hostages, especially Mike, Bob, and Rachel. I thank each of them individually for being there for me: Mike for his humor and ability to keep me laughing; Bob for his insight into a bigger world I knew little about; and Rachel for being our translator, allowing us to communicate with our captors. These moments are bittersweet because I'm not sure if I will ever see any of them again. Still, I exchange phone numbers and addresses with them and others—because if I've learned one thing, it's that life is unpredictable.

About 6:00 p.m., we touch down at JFK. A TWA representative comes on board and informs us we will not need to go through immigration and customs. He explains there are two rooms available to us once we get off the plane—one where our immediate families and friends will be and another where there will be news reporters. Still charged from the encounter with Nixon, I head into the press room first. But this is no orderly chance to make a statement or answer polite inquiries. Under the hot television lights, microphones are shoved in my face from all directions. At least a hundred reporters are gathered, and they shout a rapid succession of questions, similar to the ones we were asked in Cyprus:

"How did the Palestinians treat you? Did you have enough food? Why did they let you all go? Were you frightened?"

After so much time closed off from the world, I feel as if vultures are descending on me and picking over my bones, hungry for crumbs and juicy tidbits. I shake all over and my legs buckle. Someone catches me before I collapse and helps me to the exit. If I had found my voice, I might have said that the PFLP treated us humanely—under the circumstances—that despite their limited resources they managed to keep us alive, both on the plane and during the civil war. I might have said I came to see them as people, not just as terrorists, and I had more understanding of what the Palestinians had experienced over the years. And I might have said that I was scared out of my mind most days, fearing for my life, and it was my fellow hostages that kept me going.

But the experience was too raw, my thoughts too unformed.

As I regain my composure, the truth is, I don't yet know how I feel. Perhaps I'm fearful of repercussions from my family or my community if I appear even a little sympathetic to the Palestinians. Or perhaps I'll emerge from this braver than I was before. I've been on a supersized roller coaster for a couple of weeks, and my feet have just touched the ground.

In the second room, about two hundred relatives and close friends of my fellow hostages are waiting. Outside, several hundred college-aged students—mostly young men in skullcaps and women, from religious universities, in conservative dress—are gathered to welcome their classmates. They wave signs with hostages' names on them. One sign carried by a young woman makes me laugh: "We welcome home David and Shoshana from a Relaxing Vacation Overseas." The group of students and well-wishers boisterously sing Hebrew songs. I register the lyrics of the popular "Havenu Shalom Alecheim": "We welcome you home in peace." Many wave small blue and white Israeli flags.

I move through the crowd of families until I find my mother, father, and sister. They are all in tears—as I am—as we gather in a close hugging circle. I kiss each of them, not wanting to let go. It's sinking in that I'm finally home, back in the United States. I'm alive, safe, surrounded by family who love me. The terror of being a hostage is behind me. In this moment, worry falls away, like trees dropping leaves in the fall.

Around the room, my fellow ex-hostages are embracing their loved ones. I recognize some of the families—David's mother and three siblings were on the plane before their release at the end of the first week; Ben's wife, four children, and father-in-law, who had been traveling with him, are all here. I see Bob with his wife and an elderly couple who I imagine are his parents. Rachel, Shoshana, and Susan are surrounded by siblings and family. My heart is full of happiness for everyone.

RETURN TO BROOKLYN

LATE SEPTEMBER

On the drive home to Brooklyn, irrational fears pop into my head in momentary flashes: land mines on the Long Island Expressway, snipers hiding behind bushes. Memories of our final drive to freedom in Amman. Of course, I don't share these thoughts with my family. But I am disturbed that they have followed me home.

My father parks the car next to the cherry tree at the end of our narrow driveway. I enter our house from the back porch, and Joel, my older brother, greets me in the kitchen. I'm glad he didn't come to the airport; Mother probably banned him from going. As a person living with schizophrenia, his behavior can be erratic.

Unshaven, Joel is wearing a white ribbed sleeveless undershirt, which hangs on the stooped shoulders of his lean six-foot body. His wrinkled khaki trousers are haphazardly rolled up to midcalf, accenting his well-worn flip flops. At twenty-eight, he looks—and behaves—like an old, troubled man.

"Hi, Mimi," he begins, bending to give me a quick hug and an awkward peck on the cheek. "Welcome home." I already know what comes next will be a barrage of questions from his limited repertoire of topics: food, restaurants, and toilets.

He flicks at his crew cut with his thumb and second finger as if to remove a pesky insect. Sure enough, he asks, "How was the food?" Joel blurts his questions in rapid fire, not waiting for a response, as if to get them out before he forgets them. "Did you eat American food? What were the bathrooms like?"

"Not much food," I answer wearily. "Definitely not American food. We had pita bread, jam, hard-boiled eggs, and sardines." It will be a long time before I can bear to eat those foods again, if ever.

"Pita? What's that? Some Arab thing? What does it taste like?" He flicks his hair again. "Is it like challah we eat on Shabbos?"

"Not really."

"And the toilets?"

I have to chuckle at Joel's focus on the basics of life. I have never understood how he sees the world, because conversations with him have been difficult. Yet now I can relate to him in a way I could not before. Stripped of personal agency, we, too, focused on these fundamentals in captivity. How many daydreams and conversations did we share, as hostages, about our longings for familiar foods and a clean bathroom? Joel's limited life experience is structured around these most human concerns.

My mother intervenes. "Joel, why don't you let Mimi settle in? She's tired from her long travel. You can talk later."

"Okay, Ma," he replies, accepting her silencing as he always has. He sits at the pink Formica kitchen table and stares into space. He always calls her *Ma*. Debi and I call her *Mother*, preferring the formal title that better captures the distance in our relationship.

During my childhood, our house always seemed big. As a teenager, the inside of the house—the only house I'd ever lived in—seemed smaller. But now, compared to the crowded, small spaces I've been held in over the past few weeks, our house appears expansive.

I retreat upstairs to the security of my bedroom, close the door, and cry for what our group of hostages experienced, for the maimed and orphaned Palestinian children, and for the desperate mother who wanted us to take her baby. During captivity, showing my emotions might have affected the morale of the whole group. Now that I'm alone, I can let my raw emotions flow. I have only myself to think about. And, apparently, I still have a lot to process.

I take my third shower as a free person, elated once again by abundant hot water and, this time, the addition of my favorite products: Camay soap, Breck shampoo and conditioner, a Lady Gillette razor, all of which I took for granted before. Best of all, I have a closet full of clothes, a drawer with clean underwear, and my own toothbrush. My contact lenses got blown up with the planes, so ordering a new pair and getting these glasses off my face is a top priority.

The smell of fried onions in my mother's noodle casserole and the sautéed almonds in the green beans draws me to the kitchen. We all sit around the table, including Debi, who is taking a few days off from work so she can be at home with the family. Joel's sitting with us but he's having leftover roast chicken, one of the few foods he eats.

My parents do not ask many questions about my time in Jordan. Maybe they think they understand what happened from reading the *New York Times*, listening to Walter Cronkite on the CBS nightly news, and receiving occasional updates from the State Department and the airlines. Maybe they just want me to rest. Or maybe they don't know how to talk to me about such a delicate topic. We've never discussed anything real. I tell them some of the story, but I skip my fears of rape and death. I don't tell them about the whistling bombs in Amman. I'm not intentionally concealing details; I want to put them aside. But I know what kind of discussions are acceptable in our household. It's not as if we're silent with one another—Debi and I have always talked with our mother, but mostly about things that aren't deeply emotional and personal. We laugh and make light of most matters, even serious ones, keeping pain unspoken and as far as possible from where we sit. We can't joke about the hijacking, so we avoid it.

I leave room for dessert, the most important part of any meal. My mother has bought my favorite desserts from Ebinger's—one of her ways of showing love. I devour an Othello, an egg-shaped sponge cake filled with chocolate butter cream topped with a thick chocolate coating. I'm in heaven. I have not lost my faith in the healing properties of chocolate.

Filled with my favorite foods, I excuse myself to return to my bedroom and lie on my bed for the first time in four months. Though I am physically exhausted, my mind is hyperactive, replaying moments on the plane and in the apartment like a movie on an endless loop. The angry eyes of the scar-faced guerrilla as he warns that the PFLP can find me anywhere. The crumpled, smoky shells of airplanes after the explosions. The plumes of black smoke filling the sky.

The black phone on my mother's dresser rings late into the night. Journalists from around the world seek first-person accounts of my experience. I tell my mother—the designated phone answerer—to always say I'm sleeping. I'm reluctant to repeat the scene from the airport and fear reporters' questions will force me to relive parts of the ordeal before I'm ready.

The next day is Rosh Hashanah, the Jewish New Year, when we are all expected to be at home and attend synagogue. But this year, I'm too upset to be in public. Not yet anyway. My parents understand my request to stay home, and I ask them to say prayers for me. I can't face the onslaught of questions from well-intentioned friends of the family. I'm disoriented and crave solitude and time to get my bearings.

I have questions for myself, too. How do I feel about being Jewish now? Do I have any interest in practicing my religion? It's too big a question to consider at this moment, but being a hostage in Jordan has deepened the breach between me and my faith that dates back to my early teens.

As I'm pondering these questions, my mother enters the room. "Are you feeling better now?" she asks. It seems like a rather naive question—as if my anxiety could miraculously vanish after a few hours—and I have a feeling that was just an opener.

"Feeling good after dinner. It's great to be home."

"I have an idea that I want to share with you," she says excitedly. "I'd like the two of us to take a four-day trip to the Virgin Islands after Rosh Hashanah. It'll be good to be together and for you to relax on a beautiful beach before you go back to college."

"That sounds amazing. Let me sleep on it and I'll tell you how I feel in the morning," I say, unsure if I want to travel again so soon. Then I share another concern. "I've already missed about three weeks of classes. I'm not sure if I can miss even more."

"Think about it. We'll talk tomorrow. It's your choice. I hope you decide to go," she says, leaving the room.

Today it is understood that when a person is released from a hostage situation, they will need a transitional period to adjust to "normal" life. Typically, newly freed hostages go into an inpatient facility for a period of decompression, evaluation, and treatment for physical and mental health issues before they go home to their families. With support from trauma specialists, this provides a time for ex-hostages to readjust. This was not the case in 1970.

Later that evening, I talk about my experience to my sister, who asks gentle questions and doesn't probe deeply. She's already commented on how much weight I've lost. I share how exposed I felt in my minidress, how I got my period, and my fear that the guerrillas might harm me and other young women on the plane. I know I can share anything with her—we've been doing it all our lives.

Debi was raped by a stranger when she was sixteen while walking Pepi, our black French poodle. She was just a few houses away from ours when it happened; it was dusk and the stranger forced her into an alley. My mother didn't call the police; she didn't want the neighbors to know. Our family doctor, whom she trusted with our secrets, made a house call to examine her. I was only ten years old, but my sister's experience planted a seed of fear of strange men in me. It also cemented a familiar pattern: that personal and traumatic events in the family were to remain hidden and unspoken.

"Did the guerrillas touch any of the women?" Debi asks. "Did you have any way to protect yourself?" These were questions our mother would never ask. There was no talking or even joking about sexuality in our house. It didn't exist. We wondered how we were ever conceived.

Three years ago, the summer after my freshman year in college, I was living at home, working at Wonder Bread in Lower Manhattan, answering phones and filing. One day I came home to find my mother fuming.

"Slut!" she snarled. "Whore! You're lucky I'm letting you in the house." I wasn't sure what she was talking about until I spotted my pink diary open on the kitchen table next to her. It had been well hidden—or so I thought—in my underwear drawer. Of course, I'd written about sleeping with guys at college; it was supposed to be private.

"If you're going to act like a tramp," she barked, "we won't send you back to GW. You'll have to transfer to Brooklyn College and pay for it yourself."

Grabbing my diary, I stormed out of the room. It seemed better not to respond. What could I possibly say to get out of this one? Usually, when I didn't behave as she expected, she gave me the chilling silent treatment for days, not even looking at me, erasing me from her sight. "The ice queen cometh," I mumbled in anticipation. Sure enough, Mother left for Philadelphia the next morning, and we never talked about the diary again. Ever. And that fall, I went back to GW. That's how we dealt with conflict in our house. Shoved it back into the underwear drawer.

So it's no wonder Debi is the only one asking if I had any way of defending myself on the plane. "A spoon and a butter knife were all we had for protection," I tell her. "Most of the time we were in a group, and there were men with us. But there were a few times when it was only women. Then it got scary. The whole thing was scary, Deb."

She pulls me into her arms and gives me a kiss. "I'm so glad you're home. I missed you so much—worried about you all the time. I couldn't be in this family if you weren't with me."

I hug her back tightly. "I love you too, Deb."

As I lie in bed and try to sleep, Joel is in the bathroom next door making noises. I've listened to his mysterious soundscape for years, mostly when the rest of the family slept and I was reading Nancy Drew and, later, Daphne Du Maurier. Now, Joel's unintelligible speech, hissing, and muffled laughter filters through the thin wall. He's talking to his imaginary audience in a language I don't understand. Sometimes his sounds are blocked for a few moments by a flushing toilet or running water. Covering my ears with pillows and sinking deep under the covers is useless.

I know I can't sleep if I continue to think about Joel. He's out of the bathroom and the house is quiet. Instead, I consider the proposal my mother made that evening. She seems worried about my health and wants me to have a few restful days in a beautiful setting. Being by the ocean is always soothing. There's a part of me that can't believe she's even suggesting my getting on a plane again—but the prospect of being on a magical beach beside tranquil blue waters is alluring. Maybe having something to look forward to is good for me. I decide to go.

I suspect that as much as my mother wants *me* to get away, *she* also needs to leave, a break after the stress and anxiety of recent weeks. Though my father shared her worries during my time being held hostage, he still returned to work in Philadelphia, leaving the day-to-day efforts to fight for our release on my mother's shoulders. Afraid and alone at home, she made countless phone calls to members of Congress, New York state senators, the governor, the State Department, TWA, our rabbi, and members of her local Hadassah group. She contacted other families whose children were hostages. She spoke to Debi and other family members several times a day and waited for telegrams or phone calls to update her on new developments. Most of her attempts were futile, but keeping busy was her coping strategy.

My hijacking destabilized my mother. For as long as I can remember, keeping reality under control and under wraps has been her highest priority. Her opening question whenever she called me at college was, "Is everything under control?" I'd respond, no matter what, "Everything's fine." It was the expected answer, so I gave it. But her question left me wondering, were we ever in control of everything? Would we want to be? I don't want to live a predictable life.

After the Jewish New Year holiday, my mother and I visit our family doctor because I'm still lethargic, weak, and anxious. She tells me I look too thin, which surprises me because she's a constant dieter who can never be thin enough. The doctor confirms I've lost twenty-five pounds during my captivity and gives me a high-dose Vitamin B12 injection to increase my energy. He also prescribes a tranquilizer. Without a good night's sleep, it's hard to function. Illness has always softened my mother, and this time is no different. I suppose we're both softer in some ways and harder in others than we were before my ordeal.

Before we head to the Virgin Islands, I'm still not ready to talk to friends, so I'm mostly on my own. It bothers me that although the PFLP held me hostage, I still know little about them. Did they achieve their goals? I witnessed Jordan's civil war but still don't understand the forces behind it or the impact of the war on the PFLP and the region. I'm not even sure who started the war, or if that is a relevant question. Aware of my naivete about world politics, especially the Middle East, I decide to read the clippings my parents collected from the *New York Times*, the *New York Post*, and *Time*, *Life*, and *Newsweek* in the weeks I was held in Jordan.

I gather the papers from a mahogany table in the TV room and carry them to my sister's old bedroom in the attic, where I can read them in private. It's ten o'clock in the morning, and I'm still in my pale pink baby doll pajamas, a relic of my high school days. The house is quiet. Joel never goes to the attic, so I'm sure he won't suddenly appear with his penetrating questions.

A week-old *Time* magazine is on top of the pile. "Pirates in the Sky" is the cover story, in bold lettering accented by a red border. Two color photos taken at Revolution Airport are shown, one of the TWA and Swissair planes on the desert runway. The wooden ladder and the pickup truck reveal our only entry and exit points from the plane. Another photo shows passengers gathered on the desert floor. It was taken on the second day, but passengers already look disheveled. I recognize a few of them and am relieved not to see myself in the photos. It's a strange sensation to view these events from afar, to imagine myself a spectator, someone who's just reading the news. But it's all so real and so raw to me.

The magazine features black-and-white pictures of the planes after they were blown up, the smoldering wreckage visible through a smoky fog. Jubilant guerrillas pose atop the engines of the wrecked jets. The

THE HIJACK WAR

FIGS. 14A AND 14B. Magazines and newspapers around the world covered the hijackings, which marked the first extended hostage situation in aviation history. These *Newsweek* and *Time* covers appeared on September 21, 1970. Author's collection.

FIFTY CENTS
SEPTEMBER 21, 1970
TIME
Pirates in the Sky

CLASS OF SERVICE
This is a fast message unless its deferred character is indicated by the proper symbol.

WESTERN UNION
TELEGRAM

SYMBOLS
DL = Day Letter
NL = Night Letter
LT = International Letter Telegram

The filing time shown in the date line on domestic telegrams is LOCAL TIME at point of origin. Time of receipt is LOCAL TIME at point of destination

KH28 1 623P EDT SEP 29 70 (18)SYB355 CTC2 14 WG209
WW SNA083 CM GOVT PDB SN WASHINGTON DC 29 448P EST
FAMILY OF MIRIAM BEEBER DLY 75
1336 E. 23RD ST
BROOKLYN NY

MRS JAVITS AND I WANT YOU TO KNOW THAT WE SHARE THE TREMENDOUS SENSE OF CELIEF AND THANKSGIVING THAT MIRIAM IS HOME SAFELY AND THAT HER INCREDIBLE EXPERIENCE IS NOW A THING OF THE PAST. MAY THE NEW YEAR BRING YOU AND YOUR FAMILY HEALTH, HAPPINESS AND LONG LIFE AND PEACE TO THE WORLD
JACOB K. JAVITS US SENATOR

SF1201(R2-65)

FIGS. 15A, 15B, 15C, AND 15D. After Mimi Nichter's return home, she received many messages welcoming her back, including a telegram from Senator Jacob Javits and letters from Governor Nelson Rockefeller and TWA president F. C. Wiser. Author's collection.

STATE OF NEW YORK
EXECUTIVE CHAMBER
ALBANY 12224

NELSON A. ROCKEFELLER
GOVERNOR

September 30, 1970

Dear Miss Beeber:

May I, as Governor of New York and on behalf of the eighteen million citizens of our State, express to you our joy and relief in your safe return to your home, your families and loved ones.

I can personally testify to both the anxiety and concern of all the people of our State during the events of the past three weeks for your well-being and safety, as well as our pride in the manner with which you conducted yourselves under such hazardous circumstances.

With best wishes for the future,

Sincerely,

Nelson A. Rockefeller

Miss Mimi Beeber
1336 East 23rd Street
Brooklyn, New York

TRANS WORLD AIRLINES, INC.

605 THIRD AVENUE · NEW YORK, NEW YORK · U.S.A. 10016

PRESIDENT

September 29, 1970

Miss Miriam Beeber
1336 East 23rd Street
Brooklyn, New York 11220

Dear Miss Beeber:

I am writing to express my personal sorrow for the emotional suffering you experienced as a result of the infamous act of air piracy which occurred to our Flight #741 on September 6. I am most grateful that you have finally been returned safely. I would also like to commend you for the courage with which you faced this most distressing experience. I sincerely hope that throughout you were aware that the people of TWA were doing everything possible to alleviate your discomfort.

The events of September 6 and since have caused in responsible men the world over feelings of indignation and outrage, coupled with a sense of relief that most of those innocently involved have been spared. While our immediate goal is to attain the prompt release of the remaining six passengers being held in Jordan, we will not rest until the skies are made safe for all people in peaceful pursuit of their right to travel wherever and whenever they wish, without threats to their safety and well-being. Surely governments and their leaders now realize that only through joint action can this be accomplished, that the punishment for such a crime must be so severe as to deter any future hijacking, that human lives and property cannot be exposed to individuals and groups seeking notoriety for selfish ends. People are not pawns. They should not and must not be subjected to illegal seizure, to be held for indeterminate periods against their will.

Speaking for TWA, I assure you of our dedication to this goal. We shall perservere for as long as it takes for sanity to return to the minds and hearts of men of all nations. The episode has been a shocking and, hopefully, an awakening experience.

Miss Miriam Beeber September 29, 1970
Page Two

The time for meaningful action is now. We cannot wait any longer. We ask for the support of all people, all governments, in the finding of a lasting solution to this inexplicable phenomenon of human behavior.

We are confident that the solution will be found. None of us will soon forget those incredible days of anxiety; indeed, we should not be permitted to forget. We must remember, to ensure that it will never again happen.

Sincerely,

F C Wiser

F. C. Wiser

image is vivid in my mind, but I'm glad others can see it now, too. I try to remember where the photographers were standing, but I was so mesmerized watching the planes blowing up, I did not register their presence.

I also discover several telegrams and letters that were sent from the TWA president and New York State officials.

Downstairs, the phone rings.

"Mimi," my mother calls from the base of the attic stairs. "A journalist from a German magazine, *Stern*, is on the phone. Do you want to take it?"

"Nope. Not doing interviews." These articles leave me feeling like a story, not a person. As a hostage I felt like a pawn, not an individual with free will. Now I need to reclaim my personhood and reestablish my sense of self.

As I continue to read, my fears during captivity are confirmed in unsettling ways; we were right in believing we were close to death. There was no one looking for us. No rescuers knew where we were. It was a miracle that we had all come home physically unharmed. The psychological toll had not yet emerged.

In the final days of our captivity, the U.S. government asked Israel to join Britain, West Germany, and Switzerland to offer a deal: The seven Palestinian guerrillas imprisoned in Europe plus two Algerians in Israel would be freed in exchange for all the hostages. While the fine print of the arrangements was being resolved, the PFLP were to move all hostages to a safe place.

One day before our release, the Jordanian army discovered the European hostages in the Wahdat refugee camp. Their guards had abandoned them to fight elsewhere in Amman. When Jordanian soldiers approached the house where they were being held, the Europeans ran outside, shouting they were British, Swiss, and German hostages, and were "rescued." Now I understood why they never called our families; they had just been moved to another location in Amman.

When the news of their release was announced, the world learned none were Americans. The PFLP realized if the American hostages were also found and accidently rescued, their remaining bargaining power would be forfeited. Our group of thirty-two was released, but six Americans held elsewhere were still unaccounted for. This group was finally released and came home safely a few days after we did.

The PFLP provided names of more than fifty prisoners they wanted released from Europe and Israel in exchange for all the hostages now returned to their countries. They promised if the exchange was accomplished, they would not engage in future hijackings. Britain freed hijacker Leila Khaled, the woman whom the two PFLP sisters, Laila and Nadia, so admired and hoped to emulate. Switzerland and West Germany released the fedayeen in their prisons. Israel released none. In all, *only seven prisoners* were released and flown to Egypt, where they were celebrated by PFLP comrades.

The newspapers' accounts astonished me. I was grateful all the hostages had come home and none had been wounded or killed, despite having been in the middle of a combat zone for more than ten days. Despite my fears while being held against my will in a foreign country, I had never appreciated the chaos surrounding us, the political implications, or the full extent of our danger.

In the end, what had been achieved? The release of seven guerrillas imprisoned in Europe did not seem like a great success to me, but then what was *their* measure? Not being dismissed as marginal, their liberation movement was now recognized worldwide. The plight of the Palestinians was news for weeks. Perhaps that was the success they had hoped for.

I realized how little I knew of the world and that I wanted to know more. My wounds from the hijacking were raw and open, but they had also prepared me for a complex and nuanced understanding of the world and perhaps my place in it.

FINDING REFUGE

FALL 1970–SPRING 1971

It's a crisp fall morning and yellow and red leaves are piling up around the neighborhood. My mother and I are in a taxi to the airport for our trip to the Virgin Islands. My stomach is queasy thinking about the flight. It's been only two weeks since I've been home from Jordan, and I'm about to get on a plane again. Am I crazy to have agreed to this trip?

Despite the spate of hijackings, JFK airport is not yet equipped with metal detectors. What dangers lurk? In the lounge for the flight to Saint Thomas, I pick up and put down the Herman Hesse book I've brought, leaf through an out-of-date magazine, and compulsively inspect the other passengers just in case they're terrorists.

At this point in my life, my mother is an unlikely travel partner. We've never been close, and I hope being alone together might bring us closer. I don't understand why she avoids what I believe are deep, meaningful topics of conversation. She bears the weight of the responsibility of caring for my brother while keeping his problems hidden from extended family and community members. I remember a college friend telling me her mother put on an "emotional girdle" when she left home that compressed her negative feelings and enabled her to smoothly interact with others. My mother, too, wears that kind of girdle. My friend and I, along with so many of our generation, are different from our mothers: anti-rules, anti-bras (and girdles), anti-war, and pro drugs, sex, and gender fluidity.

The boarding announcement brings me back to the anxious moment. On the plane, I watch for sudden movements of passengers and listen for threatening sounds, but my vigilance is unneeded, and the flight proceeds uneventfully. As the plane makes its final descent to St. Thomas, the sea below is dotted with fishing boats, and I remind myself we are soon to arrive at a peaceful place, far from any desert.

After driving through the capital, Charlotte Amalie, our taxi ascends a mountainous road with an expansive view of the Caribbean. Sweet-smelling air streams through our windows. After twenty minutes, we descend into an isolated bay, with one hotel called Frenchmen's Reef dominating the landscape. There's a large swimming pool surrounded by palm trees and a semicircular building set back from the water's edge. My mother read about this new hotel in the *New York Times*. The article raved about the architecture and luxurious rooms. I'm definitely not used to staying in a beautiful resort; it's not our family's style or budget.

Our beachfront suite is near the bottom of the hill, with a mesmerizing view of the blue-green water. The rooms are bright and airy with a tropical theme. Glass doors offer views of the lounge chairs with colored pillows and the turquoise sea. A short path leads to a white sand beach. An unfamiliar feeling of gratitude arises toward my mother for choosing this beautiful place for our getaway. It's not high season, so the resort has few guests.

I change into my bathing suit, grab my goggles, and walk to the water's edge. The sea is as warm and calm as bathwater, and the stillness and bright sunlight make the underwater visibility excellent. I swim slowly, diving to observe schools of colorful fish flitting over the reef, savoring the silence.

When I emerge, my mother is sitting on a chaise lounge reading a local newspaper.

"Want to put that paper down and come for a swim? The water's amazing!" I suggest, reaching for a towel.

"I'm enjoying looking at the water. I'm not much of a swimmer," she says. I know that but hope to nudge her to try something new. Aren't we here to let go? My father loves the ocean and occasionally, when he was home in New York, took me to a crowded Long Island beach. When I went out with my mother, it was to Manhattan to visit a museum or to shop. She is excited by art and opera, while my father savors trees and flowering plants. They share few interests and live physically separate lives.

"Come on," I urge. "Wade to your knees. The water is so warm. I'll go in with you—it'll be fun." Despite my pleading, she declines. The rest of my afternoon is spent alternating between swimming and lounging, enjoying the freedom of luxuriating in the warm sunlight after weeks of captivity in dark, fear-filled spaces.

In the evening, we have a delicious fish dinner at the hotel. My mother rarely drinks alcohol, but we enjoy pina coladas to celebrate my return home and share a slice of chocolate cream pie.

She shares again how painful and frightening my captivity was for her, especially when the planes were blown up. First, she received a call from the State Department informing her that *all hostages* had been safely released and were in Amman. Then, a few hours later, she received a second call, with news that *I was not* among the passengers who were in Amman and my whereabouts were unknown. She believed she would never see me again.

I know how hard it is for her to talk about her emotions. Probably the combination of alcohol, chocolate, and sunbathing allowed her to open up as much as she did. I don't ask my mother questions about my father's role in receiving and processing all this news, but I suspect she is angry with him for not being more involved. She is always angry with him.

I tell my mother that I've read the articles she saved, and how being a hostage was so different from what was described. I hope this will prompt her to ask questions about my experience but, to my great disappointment, she doesn't. I know that she's not equipped to listen to the real story, so maybe it's better that I don't tell her.

She believes I should forget about what happened and get on with my life; returning to college and attending classes will be a good distraction while I readjust. Her advice—if I can call it that—doesn't make sense to me: It's not like my experience will dissolve like salt in water.

The next morning, black clouds gather, and thunder rumbles in the distance. The sea has changed from calm to angry. The turbulence and dark sky make the water murky, the azure blue now a dull gray. Hotel staff warn that a tropical storm is moving toward St. Thomas. Storm surges of four to five feet are forecast, and heavy rain and flooding are expected. The staff boards up windows and brings lounge chairs indoors. We want to leave, but all flights are canceled.

Which is how I find myself stuck inside with danger encroaching outside. Again. Lightning bolts shoot across the sky. Thunder strikes sound like bombs. The wind howls, the temperature drops, and I slide under the covers. Unnerved, I cry. I have never been in a tropical storm, but being scared and out of control is all too familiar.

My earlier calm quickly morphs into anxiety. I'm no longer here in this beach resort, I'm hurtling back to the apartment in Amman, running into the hall to take cover. Is this what the future holds for me? Will my present continue to be hijacked by the past? I don't want to live in that future.

During breakfast, sheets of rain fall—huge raindrops so different from the drizzle I'm used to in New York. We dash back to our room. For the next two days, rain smashes against our glass doors with such force that I worry they may shatter.

I feel a creeping anxiety as the hours pass; I worry the wind-driven seawater will flood our room. Our tranquil interlude has been broken. My mother reads a James Michener novel and eventually falls asleep, snoring with her mouth open. Like at home, she has found a way to block out the intensity of what's going on around her.

At nightfall, the storm abates, but the island has lost power, and the hotel backup generator is broken. We eat a simple meal at the hotel and return to our room with candles.

By the next afternoon, the winds and intermittent rains dissipate enough for me to walk on the beach. The pristine raked sand is now littered with fallen palm fronds, snapped tree branches, tender coconuts, and garbage. There have been no serious injuries or deaths from the storm; property damage, though intense, has not been as devastating as was anticipated. Nonetheless, our dip into paradise has come to an abrupt end.

We leave the Caribbean on the first available flight to New York.

But the time away has succeeded in making me eager to get back to college to reconnect with friends and get back to classes. I worry how I'll catch up on the month I've missed. I call my roommate, Karen, to let her know when I'll arrive. We talk about her summer in DC, but when she asks about the hijacking, I say we'll talk about it when I get back.

Three days later, I travel by train from New York to Washington. As I climb the stairs to our one-bedroom brownstone apartment, I feel a surge of happiness. The door to the apartment is slightly ajar, and I'm greeted by a loud "Surprise!" Karen has invited two of our close friends, Annie and Eileen, to welcome me.

Karen envelops me in a hug. "I've missed you. It's been way too long." Her dark hair frames her narrow face, and she's wearing her favorite overalls and Grateful Dead T-shirt.

Annie, in a black miniskirt and purple peasant blouse, kisses me on both of my cheeks. "It's so good to see you. Are you okay?" She steps back for a moment and inspects me head to toe. "Wow! You're *sooo thin.* Is that from bad food on the kibbutz or the hijacking?"

I brush it off, hoping she won't ask more questions. "The hijacking, you know, not much to eat."

"Not to worry," she says, grinning. "You're as cute as ever."

Eileen is tan, as always, and is wearing a fitted black T-shirt, black bell-bottoms with embroidery along the sides, and a red macramé headband. We kiss, hug, and plop down on our battered blue sofa, which we found last semester in a nearby alley. An Indian bedspread with a large red and blue mandala hangs on the wall above it. Beers, Marlboros, and Doritos are on the makeshift table, a slab of wood on cinder blocks. After a beer and getting caught up on new romances among our friends, Karen asks, "So what happened over there? We really want to know. Tell us the story."

My jaw clenches. I *don't want* to tell the story. And, hell, since when is it *a story*? It's my life. I want to *be here now*, not go back there. But I can't say that. I don't know why.

"It was total chaos—frightening—not knowing what would happen next. The moods of the guerrillas kept changing. We had to sit on the plane for a whole freaking week."

"They were *real revolutionaries*, right? Fighting for what they believed in. That's pretty far out," Eileen says.

"Well, you can call them that," I say slowly, "or you can call them terrorists. I was scared, being around them and their guns."

"Why'd they keep you for so long?" Karen asks. "The *GW Hatchett* said you were one of only five women held for the whole time. What'd they want with you?"

The question catches me off guard. Our college newspaper wrote about this—*about me*? My spirits fall, realizing that lots of people on campus will know. This isn't the only time I'll have to try to explain what happened to my peers. "They thought I was in the Israeli army because I was young and had some pictures with army friends. Pretty crazy, huh? Me, a soldier?" I shake my head. "They found an army shirt in my backpack, which was all the proof they needed. I told them I didn't believe in war, but they wouldn't listen."

I take the first opportunity to shift the conversation to life at GW, inquiring about each of their summers. When Karen and I spoke over the phone, she confided she had broken up with Gary, her longtime boyfriend. Despite their fun times together, Karen knew something was missing in the relationship. Now, she's depressed and lonely. Maybe focusing on her problems will help me forget about my own.

As our friends are leaving, Annie grabs my hand. "I'm having a party at my place day after tomorrow. You better be there!"

"I hope I can make it," I say, wondering if I can party again. Can I make small talk, smile, and laugh with others now? These skills came easily to me but, in my current state, I'm unsure how I'll function. I should tell Annie I'm not sure I'm ready for a party, but I doubt she'll understand. I'm still a little unmoored by my friends calling my captors *far out*. Anyway, I maintain a shred of hope I'll feel more confident in a few days.

The next day, I head to campus to attend classes. I stop in front of the Student Union, disoriented, studying my schedule, trying to figure out where my class is being held. Within minutes, friends and acquaintances gather around me, hugging and welcoming me. My celebrity is unsettling.

What happened over there? How was your experience? Are you okay now? What was it like being with revolutionaries? Who were they and what did they want with you?

Some students want to understand what happened, like I've had some kind of adventure. Others seem awed by the hijackers, which I find ironic because they know neither the name of the group that hijacked the planes nor their goals. They think the PFLP guerrillas are heroic, referring to them, as Eileen had, as *real revolutionaries*, heroes willing to die for their cause. By extension, I've become a hero, too, either because of my contact with them or because I've survived. They think being a prisoner must have been exciting.

In the days that follow, friends are suddenly proud to introduce me to others as "somebody who's hung out with Palestinian revolutionaries." I bristle at the implication that it was something I chose. I also know this is a naive characterization of the hijacking and the PFLP, borne of a lack of understanding and fanciful imaginations. But it's strange, wondering if I'd have reacted the way my friends are if this ordeal had happened to someone other than me. It makes me see my former self in a new light.

And it's strange that I wanted nothing more than to get back here, but the sense of belonging I once felt is gone.

There are some students at GW who are involved with anti–Vietnam War activities as members of the New Left who identify with *all* third world liberation struggles, Palestinians included. For these students, support for global revolution is part of their radical identity. Some are Jewish but challenge the notion that Israel is a progressive socialist nation. They view Israel as an enemy of the people, a Zionist country created and maintained by Western imperialism. While this pro-Palestinian stance is not embraced by my group of close friends—at least not to my knowledge—some of these ideas may have filtered into popular rhetoric and led to comments about the cool revolutionaries who had hijacked planes and taken hostages to liberate their country.

The classes I'm registered for are mostly required for my English literature major. I'm thankful they're large so I can remain anonymous. Concentrating in class is difficult, and I struggle to make sense of the lecture material and take coherent notes. Having already missed a whole month of classes, I'm worried about failing upcoming exams. I have a math test in two weeks, and it's a class that's required for graduation. I've lost confidence in my ability to understand the material.

In the weeks following my release, my mind does not settle. Talking about the ordeal trivializes it, so I withdraw from interaction with friends. I'm untethered from the world I was connected to before the hijacking. I'm a jigsaw puzzle that was once assembled but has lost some of its pieces.

Writing in my diary becomes one time when the pieces don't need to be in place, where I can rant and ramble. Below is an excerpt from that time:

> October 31, 1970
>
> It's been over a month since I've been back. My captivity has ended, but I'm not all here. I have these down vibes, coming from deep inside me. I want to hang out and rap with my friends like I used to, but when I'm with them and listen to their conversations, it's so meaningless.

I enjoy the fun we have getting stoned together, laughing at silly moments of life. But I'm full now with a world-awareness sadness. That's a world my friends don't know about, or at least we've never talked about it.

I'm thinking about Albert Camus's book *The Stranger*. Seeing it all, wanting to be part of it, and yet not really fitting in. Looking out of barred windows from his prison cell, longing to feel the sun's warm rays. Just a month back, I too was also living behind barred windows, imprisoned. Smelling war, seeing death.

Writing these words brings wet drops on my cheeks. It's raining outside too, tears of the sky falling on the roof.

Every day since I've been free, so to speak, or at least not a prisoner, I've been asked the same question, "What was it like to be a hostage?" Sometimes I answer how I remember it—the confusing chaos that filled the long hot days—and sometimes I go off on a short emotional tangent about how we came close to death and how frightened we were. Sometimes I talk about it in an intellectual way, not that I'm any kind of intellectual. I guess I mean I talk about it in a distanced way, with complex words, the politics behind the hijacking. My friends get it when I talk about the Marxist philosophy espoused by the PFLP, the struggle between the powerful and the powerless, the striving of displaced people to get back what they've lost.

I don't think anyone can ever understand what the hijacking was all about or what happened to me. Maybe that's something about me, or maybe it's who I'm talking to. I'll put the blame on words: words that can't convey what I feel. Maybe I don't know what I feel, maybe I've already shoved the words and feelings into a secret room, and I can't bring them into the light to someone who's asked me that stupid-fucking-casual question, "*Hey, what was it like to be a hostage*?"

And another weird thing, I've heard friends say things like "it's all good, man . . . all experience is good, right?" Well, it isn't. Life is really crazy, and you can't explain to anyone what yours is about.

I hope that Mike, Rachel, and Bob are doing better than I am right now. I know I could call them and see how each, or even one, of them is feeling, but I'm such a mess, I'm not sure I have the strength to do that. And our lives together, the time we shared so intensely together, is over. We've all gone back to our separate lives, the different worlds we came from. I'm hesitant—it might feel weird to call them out of the blue.

I don't want to talk openly about hostage fears, hostage dreams, hostage nightmares, hostage Jews, hostage laughter, hostage bombings, hostage memories.

I don't want to tell this story. I want to keep it hidden.

I want to stay silent.

I've been back on campus awhile before I run into Mark, a guy I dated for a few months before I left for Israel. Sometimes when I was picking pears on the kibbutz, songs I'd heard him play on his guitar—like America's "Horse with No Name"—played in my head. I didn't want to hear his music, but I couldn't make it go away. I interpreted it as a sign that there was something more about our relationship that was ready to unfold.

Mark's hair is long and streaked with blond, the result of a summer trip surfing in California. The ocean, especially if there are big waves, is his favorite place. I'm attracted to his swimmer's body, and his way of talking openly about his emotions, unlike me.

After a long hug, he steps back and looks at me intently. "You've got a lot going on. Why don't you come over for dinner? I'll make something special to welcome you back."

"Sounds great." He's the first person not to immediately ask me about the hijacking, though I can tell he's heard about it.

At dinner, we sit on the floor by a wooden cable spool repurposed as a table. A mushroom-shaped candle flickers. He's a vegetarian and has prepared a rice and vegetable stir fry topped with Chinese crunchy noodles. He tells me about his cross-country summer trip and surfing, and I talk about life on the kibbutz and traveling in Israel. Again, he doesn't ask for details about what happened in Jordan.

Mark's apartment and his companionship become my refuge. He's been trained to talk with Vietnam vets who are having bad LSD trips that can result in flashbacks from the battlefield, and this skill turns out to translate well to me and my trauma. His empathy soothes my disquiet mind. When I weep unexpectedly and seemingly without reason, he holds me and gently rubs my back. In those moments, a comfortable silence stretches between us.

We walk or bike to campus together, take his dog to the park, and participate in marches against the war in Vietnam and for women's liberation. Although these protests are happening across the country, Washington provides the most visible stage for voicing disapproval of U.S. government policies, with thousands congregating on the National Mall and the U.S. Capitol. People we know and their friends from around the country frequently crash on the floors of our apartments to attend these demonstrations.

One large demonstration turns violent, with protestors scattering in all directions, away from fully armed police ready to deploy tear gas. Shots are fired into the crowd, and throngs of angry people push, scream, and fight with the police. In this toxic, violent, and unpredictable situation, I have trouble holding myself together as I'm afraid a hand grenade might explode nearby.

"I've got to split now!" I tell Mark with urgency.

Sensing my panic, he grabs my hand, and we sprint to his apartment, about eight blocks away. After that, I stop going to demonstrations. I still believe in them, of course, but they compound my anxiety. Not participating in protests—regular events that bonded me to friends—further separates me from my social network.

I'm comfortable hanging out with Mark's dog, Damian, a black Scottish terrier, who shares our bed. I remember how Damian was one of my happy thoughts when I was trying to escape the reality of the apartment in Amman. Damian's presence by my side is even more reassuring now; his growling scares away anyone who gets too close. A loyal, fierce dog, he distrusts anyone in uniform, like I do.

I spend hours lying on Mark's bed listening to the bands America, Santana, and Jefferson Airplane. "White Bird," a popular song by the band It's a Beautiful Day, captures my feelings of loneliness. The song describes a white bird in a golden cage, feeling alone and unknown, knowing that she must fly, or she could die.

I identify with the white bird. Something is amiss, although I don't know how to articulate it. I have regained my physical strength, but I do not understand the psychological dimensions of healing and recovery. I do not know that trauma can linger and lodge in the body and mind. I am unable to talk about my recurring nightmares of the planes exploding and the whistling of bombs. Startled awake in a cold sweat, I try to fall back to sleep, worrying that I will again be consumed by frightening visions.

During the day, the sound of a car backfiring or the blare of a passing ambulance leaves me jittery. These are not the sounds I heard during the war, but they leave me anxious that *something else* might happen. Loud noises are one of my jolts, a small flash of panic that can consume me during the day or awaken me minutes after I've closed my eyes.

Small spaces like elevators or crowded buses also serve as triggers of my confinement on the plane. Deep breaths help me quiet my thudding heartbeat and regain a tentative sense of calm.

I think often of my mother's question: "Is everything under control?" Though it definitely is not, maybe I can pretend it is, like she does. Back on with the mask. The mask I wear when I bury my feelings and silence my voice. From the outside, it looks like everything's okay. Only I know it isn't.

PTSD was not a mental health diagnosis until 1980. Before then, the conditions that soldiers experienced after their return from war were labeled with terms like *shell shock*, *combat fatigue*, or *Vietnam stress*.

Perhaps having no idea that my anxiety would continue after my return compounded my experience. Maybe I would have recovered more quickly if someone had suggested I seek counseling or therapy. But why would they? It was expected that I'd readjust quickly. And my parents were opposed to therapy, even for my brother, who was living with schizophrenia.

The summer before the hijacking, I'd hitchhiked with my roommate to Woodstock for the festival. Was it only a year ago? Would I do something like that now? I had dreamed of living in London someday, finding work, so I could make enough money to travel around Europe to France, Spain, Portugal, and Morocco. Now I wonder if I have the courage to go far away.

At college, Karen and I talk about what we might do after graduation, but neither of us has ideas beyond getting a job that pays enough so we can move out of our parents' homes. Returning to Brooklyn and living with my parents is unthinkable. I majored in English literature because I imagined becoming a writer, but I have no idea how writers earn a living. I envision living in Manhattan with a job in a publishing house where I can work my way up from answering phones and welcoming people at the front desk to editing. I've worked in offices in Manhattan during summer vacations and have clerical skills. I'm a fast typist and know how to file papers.

My mother has frequently offered her generation's limited vision: Elementary school teaching or nursing are practical, suitable careers for girls. She hopes I'll marry soon after graduation to a Jewish medical student or doctor, a respected profession she associates exclusively with men. Nursing or teaching will provide an income until I have children; I can resume my career when the children begin school.

My boyfriend, Mark, has decided to travel through Africa after graduation and asks me to join him on his open-ended journey. I'm intrigued by his invitation, but only seven months have passed since my return from Jordan, and I still suffer unpredictable bouts of anxiety. I don't know where his journey might take him, and I worry how I'll react to people in Muslim countries. Would seeing people in head scarves or robes or hearing Arabic trigger memories of my hostage ordeal? If we were traveling in a remote region of North Africa, would I worry about being abducted? How would it feel to be in a desert again?

I'm honest with him. "Sounds great, but not sure I can handle it."

"It's like surfing," he says. "When you fall off a big wave and are held under, it can freak you out because you can't find your way to the surface. When that happens to me, I paddle in to catch my breath and get grounded. After a while, I paddle back out. I have to or I'd lose my nerve and always be afraid of surfing big waves. Push through fear or get stuck."

I don't want the hijacking to limit what I'm willing to do and steal my future. Traveling through Africa is an opportunity that might not come again, and no appealing alternative has stood out to me yet. Graduation is approaching. In spite of everything, I've managed to pass my classes. Time to make a decision is running out.

I call my sister, who usually offers sage advice.

"Moving back to Brooklyn is out of the question, and I don't want to stay in DC," I recap for her. "My friends don't understand me—they still think my hijacking was a far-out experience. It's been driving me crazy! Mark says he's gonna travel around Africa and wants me to go with him. I'm really tempted."

“Is he planning a summer trip to one or two countries or what?” Debi asks. “I need more info before offering my two cents.”

“Well, it’s not like he’s shared a planned trip with an itinerary.”

“That sounds like Mark.” She laughs. “It could get you out of the headspace you’re in, force you into the world. And if you can’t handle it, you’ll come up with another plan.”

I pause and take in her words. Maybe I’ve been waiting to see if Mark is the only one who thinks this is a good idea. “Traveling might be healing for me,” I say finally. “I mean, I’ll have to be open to . . . whatever.”

“Yeah, that’s what I’m thinking,” Debi says.

The more I think about it, the more I want to go. To educate myself, I read about the continent and learn that Africa is larger than the United States, China, and Brazil combined and comprises 20 percent of the earth’s land. I purchase a Michelin map that could be useful on the journey. There are no guidebooks to help figure out where to go or stay. We’re counting on meeting other travelers who can tell us about places they’ve been and how to get there. On our low-budget trip, we’ll use local transport or hitchhike, stay in cheap hotels or youth hostels when we are in cities; otherwise, we’ll camp out. Mark was an Eagle Scout and knows how to make a fire and cook outdoors.

I, on the other hand, am a New Yorker. My summer camp experience in the Catskills hasn’t prepared me for a trip like this. I’ve never carried a backpack on a long hike. I’ve slept outside a few times under the stars, but not in the wilderness, and certainly not in a place where I might encounter lions or tigers. I’ve also never spent a single weekend away with Mark, let alone on a different continent.

Still, I decide to trust that I’ll adjust. If I don’t like a place or it’s dangerous, we can move on. And if the Africa trip doesn’t work, I can fly back to the States.

I need a new narrative about who I am, not just to tell others, but to tell myself.

Mark has money saved and plans to set off shortly after graduation. He’s arranged for his dog to stay with his mother and younger sister, who have a large fenced yard that Damian loves, with birds he can chase.

I need two or three months to earn money for the trip, though. I find a temporary job at the Sierra Club in DC filing papers and typing memos. I enjoy learning about environmental protection and admire the large nature photographs of deep canyons, gushing rivers, and giant trees. I hope to augment my earnings with a loan from my sister. Once I have a thousand dollars, I'll be good to go. I'll buy a one-way ticket on a cheap airline to meet Mark somewhere in Europe, probably London. I also need to apply for a new passport, as I returned to the United States without one.

There is one large hurdle looming before me—my parents. I save the news of my travel plans for graduation day. After the ceremony, we celebrate with dinner at Trader Vic's, decorated with tiki statues, torches, and palm-thatched ceilings. Waitresses shimmy about in hula skirts. Our Mai-Tais arrive, frothy with pineapple juice, adorned with paper umbrellas. I'm hopeful the cocktails will smooth the conversation.

My father asks, "What are your plans?"

My next steps did not come up in our weekly phone calls, when I mostly talked to my mother. Even if we had broached the topic, I would not have revealed my travel plans any sooner than necessary.

I say innocently, "I'm going to Africa with my friend Mark." I keep my expression even, but inside I stiffen, bracing for their reaction.

"*Africa*?" my father turns crimson. The only time I've seen him like this was when I was ten and put a thick black rubber spider—the kind that came in a plastic egg from a five-cent gumball machine—in my Aunt Fay's egg salad. She shrieked, thinking it was real. I was proud of my prank, but my father grabbed the spider, threw it in the garbage, slapped my face, and sent me to my room.

"What *mishigas*!" he shouts, using the Yiddish word for foolishness or nonsense. "Nice Jewish girls from Brooklyn don't go to Africa!"

My mother looks around the restaurant and admonishes him in a low voice. "Morris, keep it down!"

I wonder if my father's anger is about my safety or about how they'll ever explain my *mishigas* to our family and neighbors. Israel, where we had relatives, seemed like a safe and appropriate place to let their twenty-year-old daughter explore—even if it didn't turn out that way—but Africa was certainly not. My parents had never traveled together beyond New York and Pennsylvania—except to Florida, a respectable place for New Yorkers to winter.

"What will you do there?" my mother asks, trying to make sense of my plans.

"Not sure. Travel, see places."

My father turns silent, but my mother persists. "See places? Like where? Africa is a very big place. How will you travel around? Where will you get the money? How long will you be gone? And who is this boy, Mark? We haven't heard you talk about him before."

My father asks the important question: "He's Jewish?"

"I'm not sure where we're going, and I don't know when I'll be back," I say. "We're going to play it by ear until our money runs out. Mark's a friend. And, yes, he's Jewish."

Over the many years since, I've often wondered why my parents never spoke to me about the potential dangers of traveling abroad so soon after my hijacking. Perhaps that aspect of the trip hadn't occurred to them yet. They were still in shock. Or perhaps they didn't know what to say, or they thought I wouldn't listen to their advice. Perhaps they thought I was old enough to make my own decisions. Sometimes they surprised me that way. I remember that shortly after my sister got her driver's license, she told my mother she wanted to go to a party and needed the car keys. It was a Friday night and our family never drove on the Sabbath. But my mother handed her the keys. "We've taught you how you should act, but you're old enough to decide for yourself."

Perhaps they thought I was mature enough, too. Somehow, I doubted it.

I was eager to leave them, their home, our country. A portal had opened, and I was ready to walk through.

ON THE ROAD

1971–1972

We traveled for sixteen months across continents, countries, and cultures. We crossed North Africa from Morocco to Egypt, journeyed down the Nile on a river barge to Sudan and East Africa, and eventually reached South Africa overland. After eight months, we traveled deck passage from Kenya to India on the ss *Karanja*, a battered British India Steam Navigation ship. We spent five months in India, journeyed overland through Pakistan, Afghanistan, Iran, and Turkey, and crossed Europe until we reached the United Kingdom. Finally, we returned to New York.

Few Americans traveled in Africa in 1971. We moved at a slow pace, taking local transportation when we could find it, walking and hitchhiking when we could not. When we met other travelers—an infrequent pleasure—we exchanged travel information, where to go and where to avoid, cheap hostels where we could shower and wash clothes, which countries required visas and how to procure them, and where to change money on the black market. U.S. dollars were valuable in Africa, and changing money outside the official banks was lucrative. In some countries, the exchange rate for dollars on the street was almost double what it was in banks. But this was a risky venture as money changers tended to be shady characters.

In remote places in Africa, it was easy to find places to camp. We carried water and food: rice, a few potatoes and carrots, tea bags, bread, and bananas. Each night, we cooked a stew on an open fire. We did not carry a tent, so we slept under a vast sky of twinkling stars. In villages or towns, we drank tea at roadside stalls, sampled local cuisine, and bought fruits and vegetables.

Most people we encountered had never met Americans before, particularly not a tall red-haired woman like me. Mark and I were frequently asked if we were married. When we said we were not, we observed people's perplexed looks. An unmarried man and woman traveling together as partners was culturally inappropriate and potentially dangerous. We decided to tell people we were brother and sister. As my brother, Mark was responsible for protecting me and our family honor. Our sibling relationship was more easily understood by those we met, who showed interest in our family and asked questions about our parents and siblings.

Throughout our travels, I moved between the worlds of women and men, although I was usually treated as invisible by men, who rarely spoke to or even looked at me. Men directed all conversation to Mark, usually in English or French. In contrast, women welcomed me into the separate worlds they inhabited, close to the hearth and close to the land. They exuded pride when they took me to their gardens to see the vegetables, fruit trees, and other crops they had planted to eat and sell in the market. Their sense of place was embodied; like the trees they tended, their families had deep roots in the earth. I remembered Laila's and Nadia's pain when they recounted their family's forced exodus from Palestine, from the land they had tended for centuries. In Africa and Asia, I was once again educated by women about the meaning of place, geography, and home.

Traveling was not always easy or fun; it was often mentally and physically demanding. Since the hijacking, I had found every border crossing fraught with real or imagined danger. My passport was on an international list of those recently stolen. At each border, I would be called into a special room and questioned. I had to explain that my original passport had been taken by the PFLP during a hijacking and that I had no idea what had become of it. The immigration inspectors questioned me, demanded details of the hijacking, and sometimes challenged my story. Each crossing left my stomach in knots. I feared some of the Arab officials might be sympathetic to the Palestinian cause. Both in Algeria and Egypt I faced intensive interrogation at entry, reviving memories of my earlier interrogations on the plane, which had been just eleven months back.

In Cairo, my body stiffened as I navigated the busy souks and bustling streets; it reminded me of the pushing and shoving of the mobs surrounding our bus in the refugee camp outside Amman. Neither the stark beauty of the Pyramids nor the Sphinx at Giza diminished my creeping anxiety. The shouts of hustlers, "Hey missus, want camel ride, need guide?" aggravated me, obliterating my appreciation of one of the Seven Wonders of the World.

Though I appreciated the physical beauty of the countries through which we passed, there was much to cause distress. In South Africa, apartheid was agonizing to witness. I observed similar separation and dehumanization of people in India, as a result of the caste system. While I understood little at the time about this layered, complex culture, I was told by people I met about the many ways in which the hierarchical caste system separated people in all aspects of their lives, including the most mundane, like whom you could eat with, or where you could obtain your water. In many countries, I observed the impact of "othering" in its various manifestations.

First as a hostage and then as a traveler living a basic lifestyle, I came to appreciate the importance of simple things: clean drinking water, a toilet, and a place to bathe. I developed a deep respect for people who survived, even thrived, with only basic resources.

The months spent on the road were full of adventure. As I'd hoped, they were healing, too. Walking helped; the simple repetitive motion of placing one foot in front of another released me from circular thoughts about my past and enabled me to more fully inhabit my body. Moving slowly helped me appreciate the beauty and diversity of the world around me. I learned patience, absorbing events and sensations as they occurred.

In Khartoum, we made friends with four young Sudanese doctors who had recently returned from their medical training in the USSR. They called Mark and me "the free people," who were able to travel the world without governmental or personal restrictions. They wanted to hear about our adventures through Africa. Sudanese citizens could not travel freely, because of financial and political restrictions. Their perception of me as "totally free" was ironically at odds with my sense of self, but it helped me to recognize the astonishing political and economic liberty I'd been afforded, despite the roadblocks my ordeal still sometimes caused. Compared to these men, I was free to travel, to dream, and to expect that my dreams would bear fruit. I didn't want to squander the advantages I had.

I carried the hijacking experience with me, but it no longer defined who I was. As a traveler, I was immersed in the present. I focused on immediate and basic concerns: eating, exploring the nuances of daily life across cultures, staying safe. Without a fixed itinerary, I relied on my intuition as a guide. In captivity, I lost individual agency and was filled with a paralyzing fear and uncertainty of what would come next.

In contrast, on the road I learned to appreciate the unpredictability and spontaneity of daily life. As I lived more fully in the present, the past had less hold over me. When I met other foreigners, I shared stories of our recent travels, rather than stories about my "real" life. The emotional pain that had lived at my edges receded into the background.

We were crossing through Pakistan when I heard that Palestinian terrorists had struck again, this time at the 1972 Summer Olympics in Munich. The Munich games were the first to be broadcast internationally on television and were billed as the "Happy Olympics." West Germany was hoping to shed its Nazi past by projecting a harmonious image to the world.

The terrorists were members of a group called Black September, named in commemoration of the Jordanian civil war of September 1970, which I had been so unwillingly immersed in. Their group was founded in 1971 to wreak vengeance on Jordan's military for the deaths of thousands of Palestinians during the civil war. In Munich, eight terrorists gained entry to the Olympic village and entered the Israeli athletes' dormitory. They immediately killed two athletes, and nine others were taken hostage and brutally beaten. Millions of people around the world watched this horror as it unfolded.

The Black September group demanded the release of their comrades imprisoned in Israel—demands like those of the PFLP during our hijacking. Their demands were not met. In response, they killed another nine Israeli athletes.

The murders both reactivated memories of my hijacking and reinforced how fortunate I'd been to return alive. My response to this attack might have been more profound had I been home with access to regular news. As a traveler, I had limited opportunities to read newspapers or watch TV. Most of what I learned about the attacks in the Olympic village was days old. The delay and the distance muted the impact of the coverage, but it was a return to a dark time for me, nonetheless.

Memories of the hijacking did surface from time to time, even on the road, sometimes due to violent events like the Munich murders but more often because of subtle internal triggers I could not anticipate or control. With the passage of time, both the intensity and frequency of the surfacing memories diminished. Fear of what had happened or might have happened no longer rendered me immobile. I became confident that my newly developing—and newly discovered— emotional strength would help me face adversity and challenges in the future.

As we neared the end of our trip, what I would do next had not yet crystallized. What I did know was that I wanted to find work and an identity that would allow me to continue my travels and explorations of the world.

THE LAWSUIT

1973–1977

Three years after the hijacking, I received a letter from a lawyer asking me to join twenty-eight other former hostages in a lawsuit against Trans World Airlines. At that time, I was living in Manhattan and studying for a master's degree in teaching English as a second language at Columbia University. Mark, who was still my boyfriend, was living in Edinburgh, Scotland, where he was pursuing a PhD in social anthropology. We maintained a long-distance relationship across the Atlantic, seeing each other every few months.

The lawyers argued that TWA's gross negligence regarding security was at least in part responsible for the success of the hijacking. El Al, for example, had already had air marshals on their flights, and that hijacking had been foiled.

An individual lawsuit had already been brought against TWA by a woman who had claimed damages for mental distress. The TWA lawyers argued that if she or any other passenger had been shot or physically injured by hijackers during the flight, the airlines may have had liability, but they denied responsibility for injuries resulting from "mental anguish and distress." The Supreme Court of the State of New York disagreed, ruling she was entitled to recover damages for "fright and distress." This was significant for our lawsuit, establishing the liability of an airline for the passengers' physical and *mental* safety and providing damages up to $75,000.

I joined the group of plaintiffs suing for damages based on both bodily and mental injuries resulting from the hijacking. The Warsaw Convention of 1929 had established uniform laws for claims arising from international aviation accidents and limited liability for air carriers, but the text of the convention was in French; the pertinent language regarding liability was "*lesion corporelle*," translated as *bodily injury*. The question at bar was whether *bodily injury* included *emotional distress*. In our lawsuit against TWA, after hearing expert testimony, the court determined that *lesion corporelle* "includes the concept of *mental injury* as a recovery for damage, *even absent* concomitant physical manifestation." My claim of mental injury included anxiety, stress, recurring fears triggered by particular settings and events, and feelings of alienation. My claim of bodily injury included extreme weight loss and irregular menstruation for years following the hijacking.

Two years after the lawsuit was filed, I was deposed. I was the last deponent to be called, because Mark and I had been living in India for two years doing anthropological research. We had married just before beginning fieldwork. While in India, Mark was doing research on health behavior in rural South India, interviewing patients, ayurvedic and allopathic practitioners, astrologers, spirit mediums—all types of healers people sought treatment from when sick. After a few months of teaching English in a rural secondary school, I joined Mark in his research, focusing on women's health. At the deposition, I was six months pregnant. I had returned to New York for a few weeks to visit my family. Mark returned to Scotland to write his dissertation.

I had talked to my lawyer, Mr. Alvin Meadow, only briefly on the phone, and he had not prepared me for the content, purpose, or setting of the deposition. We met for the first time in the law offices of TWA's counsel, an international law firm with hundreds of employees, located on the top floors of Rockefeller Plaza in New York. Mr. Meadow was an elderly man with a wrinkled face sprinkled with dark brown age spots. Mr. Egan, the TWA lawyer, was middle-aged and impeccably dressed in a well-tailored suit and polished shoes. He exuded competence. I arrived alone, tired from the long walk and subway trip from my parents' house in Brooklyn.

Mr. Egan's questions were exhausting, beginning with my checking in at the Tel Aviv airport, my six days on the plane, and what occurred afterward. About the hijacking, he began by asking, "What sort of information did the guerrillas collect from you?" I recounted that some passengers hid their passports. "How did the guerrillas show their anger? Did the guerrillas beat or hit anyone to show their anger? Were you poked with a gun or rifle while onboard?" I said I had been, and he asked whether the gun had touched my head, and for how long. I replied that I did not know, and Mr. Egan asked if I had been wearing a watch.

This line of questioning seemed absurd, and I wasn't sure if I should laugh or cry. How long a person held a gun to my head was not a fair measure of how much fear I experienced. Would ten minutes result in less fear or less harm than twenty or thirty minutes? Was there a threshold after which "harm and distress" became believable? I was insulted and sickened by the questions, and so was the baby inside me, who was kicking me in the ribs.

Mr. Egan then asked a series of questions about my menstrual cycle, which was embarrassing to discuss in a roomful of strangers. I testified that after my return from Jordan, my periods were irregular for several years. Had I sought treatment from gynecologists? I had, because I was afraid I would not be able to conceive. Mr. Egan pointed at my pregnant belly and laughed. "Well, it looks like that problem's been resolved."

"It's not that simple," I argue. "Not getting my period each month was stressful for me, especially in village India, where my husband and I lived in a multigenerational household. When a woman has her period there, everyone in her house is aware of it. She is restricted from cooking, touching others, and sleeps separately. Women in the family kept asking me why I didn't get my period and expressed concern I might not be able to have children. In India, having children is the most important outcome of marriage. A woman who doesn't have offspring is labeled a barren woman and considered worthless. My worth was questioned; people pitied me behind my back and inquired with Mark about his willingness to take another wife."

Mr. Egan was not deterred. "Did you see a doctor there?"

"Yes, I sought treatment from an ayurvedic doctor who was a specialist in women's menstrual problems. I took a bitter herbal medicine for a few months, and that restarted my period. Shortly after, I became pregnant. But I haven't forgotten the worry and agony I experienced that whole time in India."

"Have you presented bills for these doctor's visits and medicines? We'll have to see them." I agreed to turn over what I had to my lawyer, although finding receipts from village practitioners seemed unlikely.

My weight loss of twenty-five pounds during the hostage ordeal was another major topic of the deposition. I was asked how much I weighed in college, in Israel, after the hijacking, and even now as a pregnant woman. I was horrified to answer questions about my weight and to hear it discussed as if it were a meaningless number on a scale. As with many girls and women, my weight is closely tied to my sense of self. Thinness, to many women, is a prerequisite to being attractive. It's still ingrained in our culture, despite the rise of the body positivity movement. It's evident in the continual development of new weight loss programs and medications, like Ozempic. But shedding twenty-five pounds in three weeks was a dangerous consequence of inadequate food and intense fear, not the result of a crash diet.

"What's wrong with losing weight?" Mr. Egan joked. "Every woman in America would love that!" My lawyer weakly objected. I swallowed hard, holding back anger and frustration.

The lawyer asked whether I'd flown on a plane since the hijacking. "How many times have you flown and where have you gone?" He did not ask about my experience during those subsequent flights or whether I was fearful. The implication was that because I could get on a plane, I was no longer afraid to fly.

My brother-in-law, a clinical psychologist, wrote a letter on my behalf attesting that after the hijacking I suffered from anxiety, tension, fear, depression, and alienation from others. The letter was meant to document my mental and physical health in the months after the hijacking, but it wasn't enough. The TWA lawyers demanded bills from doctors, suggesting that if I had "really" suffered mental health damage, I would have sought help from a psychologist or psychiatrist. No matter that I'd been a student with no health insurance and limited finances. Shortly after the hijacking, my family doctor had prescribed medicines for me, but the airline's lawyer dismissed the prescription for tranquilizers and sleeping pills as evidence of sustained emotional injury.

"You look like a perfectly normal woman," he said. "No one would think there was anything wrong with you."

My alienation and estrangement from friends and my religion was also probed at length by Mr. Egan. Had I lit Sabbath candles before the hijacking and afterward? Did I belong to a synagogue now, and had I before the ordeal? Was I a member of Hadassah, the Women's Jewish Zionist Organization of America, before and after the hijacking? Spiritual alienation, like anxiety, must be demonstrable. As I struggled to understand and answer these questions, I noticed my lawyer had dozed off and begun to snore. Mr. Egan and I both laughed, which woke Mr. Meadow, his wrinkled cheeks turning bright red.

My momentary laughter eclipsed rising anger toward Mr. Meadow. How could he fall asleep while the biggest trauma of my life was being dissected and trivialized?

The months I'd spent on the road during my travels had helped the ground grow steadier under my feet, but my restorative journey was certainly not framed that way during the deposition. Rather, my travels in Africa and Asia, discussed briefly in establishing my activities since the hijacking, were used by TWA's lawyer as evidence I was undeterred from having adventures. Any distress I "might" have experienced had been short-lived.

By then, I knew all too well the trauma of the hijacking had left traces in my mind and body that could be reactivated given the right trigger. The deposition, which forced me to relive memories of the hijacking in excruciating detail, was the biggest trigger yet. The TWA lawyer concluded I was fine. But recounting the details had revived fear I thought I had tamed. The roiling in my gut told me that four years after the ordeal, the fear wasn't gone, only buried.

When I was a hostage, the PFLP saw me only as a Jew, a Zionist, and an American imperialist. That I might have been other than that seemed inconceivable to them. Yet again at the deposition, I felt unseen and misunderstood. Mr. Egan saw me as "perfectly normal." I'd lost weight, traveled, married, gotten pregnant. I'd performed well on simplistic gendered expectations. I'd met the metrics of female success.

I had never anticipated that the deposition would be so troubling. I'd worked hard to move beyond the hijacking, and now it burdened my heart again. Feeling sick, I pulled on my jacket and headed outdoors for fresh air. On the subway to my parents' house, my head pounded, my emotional upset magnified by the double heartbeats of the baby and me. I worried the kicking baby in my womb was also experiencing harm.

The deposition lasted two days. Afterward, I collapsed onto my childhood bed, immobilized, just as I had when I first returned from Jordan. I did not tell my mother how difficult the deposition was for me and how belittled I felt. She didn't ask many questions, and I felt certain she wouldn't understand. She would have only recited the message she had shared countless times: "Everything will be fine, you'll see." I'd already internalized her model for ignoring, or at least hiding, painful realities. If I just put the pain aside, maybe it *would* go away.

Two weeks after the deposition, my lawyer informed me that TWA had made what their lawyer had called a "generous offer" to settle out of court for $3,500. I declined.

A month after the deposition, when I was in my last trimester of pregnancy, I was hospitalized with preeclampsia, a condition diagnosed by the presence of dangerously high blood pressure that occurs most commonly among women under psychological stress. I wondered whether the stress during and after the deposition had affected my hormones and blood pressure. It was a joyous relief when our beautiful son Simeon was born healthy and normal.

My baby was two years old before I finally entered the Brooklyn supreme court building for my day in court. My lawyer had suggested my presence would make a good impression during jury selection. Shortly after I arrived, Mr. Meadow, Mr. Egan, and I were called into the judge's chamber. Because Mr. Meadow was representing our group and not just me, I was still stuck with him as a lawyer despite his lackluster performance during my deposition.

Judge Anthony Jordan was seated behind a large desk covered with papers. He motioned for us to sit. "I've been reading these papers all weekend long," he told us in a thick Brooklyn accent. "I don't care what the other judge decided in that earlier trial about this hijacking. I don't have to go with his decision that *lesion corporelle* can be interpreted as mental injury, like fright and distress, even in the absence of bodily injury."

Judge Jordan turned to me and continued: "I'll be honest with you. If you bring this to a jury, I'm 90 percent certain I'm going to tell them you can't claim on mental injury, only on bodily injury. Lady, you're not going to get anything. You better take what I can get for you—we're talking $13,000 or $15,000. If I rule that *lesion corporelle* is open to mental injury, then I open the door for hijacking cases."

I looked at him in shocked silence. Mr. Meadow said nothing.

Judge Jordan leaned back in his chair and cleared his throat. "I didn't buy the testimony of the expert witness in that previous trial against TWA. I'm an aviation buff and I can tell you that in the 1920s, when the Warsaw Convention was written, the planes were made of wood and canvas. If there was an accident, the planes burned and everyone aboard was dead. There was no question of claiming for mental injury. There wouldn't have been any."

Mr. Meadow tried to interrupt, but Judge Jordan continued. He leaned forward, pointing his finger at me. "If you bring this to trial, it's going to be postponed indefinitely. I'm a busy man and you're the mother of a young child. I'm telling you that you're going to face a lot of adjournments. Here's my calendar. Next Tuesday afternoon, I have a photoshoot for judges and that night I have a big dinner sponsored by the mayor, so that will be a short day. Then on Wednesday, we have another black-tie event for judges. So, half the week will be gone. The court will be disrupted every day."

Now I was outraged as well as shocked. I'd been a hijack hostage held by terrorists, almost gotten killed, and this judge was complaining about fancy events he needed to attend. I felt defeated, wishing I had never joined the other plaintiffs. The hijacking and hostage experience had been nightmarish, but I had eventually regained my self-confidence and had overcome many of my fears. But in the process of seeking justice, I felt denied of it. I knew in that moment that continuing was more harmful than stepping down. I would settle without a trial.

Again, talking about the hijacking with the judge brought a flood of long-suppressed memories to the surface. Weeks would pass before I regained my equilibrium. I was irritable and, though I tried to remain in the present, I continued to be distracted by random scenes of events from my time in Amman. The seeds of trauma were inside me; given the right conditions they could still flourish. If I learned one thing from the deposition experience, it's that talking about the hijacking in the wrong circumstances threatened to devastate my well-being. I wanted and needed to move on with my life and family and not spend the next month or year in court dissecting and reliving the experience.

THE JOURNEY FORWARD

In the years that followed, I was busy raising two sons, teaching cultural anthropology at the university, and publishing articles and books related to my research. During summer breaks, Mark and I would travel overseas, mostly to India and Indonesia, to work on global health projects. Our sons usually accompanied us as we wanted to raise them as world citizens who could easily adjust to traveling and living overseas. Both boys knew I had been a hijack hostage, but I never shared any details. They never asked questions, perhaps sensing my reticence. Extended family members occasionally asked me what had happened, but I evaded the question.

Like many Americans, I recall exactly where I was when 9/11 occurred and the televised footage that first aired. My sister and I were in Florida at the hospital where my mother had been admitted following a stroke. Through the lens of sadness and concern for her health, we watched the terrorist attacks unfold. My mother's last words were mumbled in response to my sister's and my horrified talk as we watched the Twin Towers crumble.

While to some Americans, the attacks may have initially appeared to be random acts of terrorism, the similarities to my experience thirty-one years earlier led me to think about it differently. Both series of hijackings were meticulously coordinated; both involved multiple simultaneous hijackings by Islamic terrorists. During 9/11, one of the planes was heroically diverted by passengers, reminding me of the brave passengers on the El Al flight in 1970 who managed to restrain one of the PFLP hijackers. In both terrorist acts, ordinary citizens were held responsible for the actions of their governments. Tragically on 9/11 thousands died; we were fortunate to all come home alive.

I mourned for the senseless loss of life. There was much to process about the unthinkable events that occurred in New York and my mother's sudden death. Though terrifying, events like 9/11 did not deter my travels and ongoing research in Indonesia, where Islamist terrorist activity was occurring. While doing fieldwork there, I occasionally felt afraid, especially if I heard about terrorist cells in nearby communities. Surrounded by local colleagues, I pushed fear aside.

In 2010 a fellow anthropologist and friend who studied war and its traumatic aftermath organized a session at the annual meeting of the American Anthropological Association. I had once talked briefly with her about my hijacking, and she thought a presentation on my experience would fit well in her session. She asked me to reflect on being in captivity in a war zone and its impact on my life. I declined, uncomfortable with the prospect of revealing my personal story to a public audience with whom I interacted professionally.

I attended her session at the conference but found that even listening to presentations by anthropologists about their experiences with terrorism moved me to tears. I barely managed to keep my outward display of emotions in check. When the session was over, I rushed out, overcome with a deep sadness I could not fully understand. My colleagues' discussion of terrorism had unleashed buried fear and a deep sense of unease. I couldn't talk about my experience in a detached and intellectualized way as my colleagues had done, but I also couldn't talk about it as a personal experience.

Finally, an experience in a yoga class made me realize that this long-buried trauma was seeking release. I'd been practicing yoga for years, but for the past few months I'd entered an intensive period of daily practice. In a heated yoga room, I was sweating profusely as I did the camel pose, an intense backbend, followed by its counterpart, the rabbit pose, a forward fold done from a seated position. While holding rabbit pose, I saw a blue ball of energy fly out of my stomach. It was jettisoned so quickly I wondered if it was real. I sensed that the "ball" was dark feelings my body wanted and needed to eject. My intuition was shouting, and I listened.

When the class was over and I rolled up my mat, I felt a euphoric sense of release. My body felt light. I recounted the experience to my yoga teacher, explaining that something had forcefully left my body during class, a negative energy I had not known was lurking inside. She did not seem surprised and explained that in yogic practice, deep forward folds can free emotional pain from our past that has become lodged in the body. Releasing this trauma offers an opportunity to resolve it.

Over the next few weeks, vivid memories from the hijacking felt as if they were emerging from my cells. And unlike other times when these memories had arisen, I observed them with interest, not fear. Still, I was curious why the release had occurred when it did, and not sooner. What had triggered it? Was it something about those poses or the yoga practice itself?

A conversation with noted yoga teacher Judith Hansen Lasater helped me understand the significance of my release. I briefly shared with her that I had been a hijack hostage for a few weeks and my earlier experience in that yoga class. She did not ask me any questions about the hijacking. But Judith suggested the release was not about yoga per se, but about the openness and vulnerability I had experienced in the class. When I asked why it had taken so long, she replied, "The body has its own time."

She asked me how I felt when I talked about the hijacking. I shared my deep sadness about the experience, how difficult it was to speak about it, and how I could not even think about it without crying.

Judith suggested that it was not the experience itself I was mourning but the loss of joy and sadness over the years—what I had lost because of my inability to express the range of my feelings. "By denying feelings of sadness," she said, "you also deny your ability to fully experience joy. By not giving voice to your feelings, you ignored the wisdom of the body. Grief is woven into the fabric of our lives. We cannot hide from it."

My experience with the hijacking has evolved over time. Many women who were brought up in the 1950s and '60s were socialized, like I was, to be private about our problems. I fully embodied my family mantra: "Don't talk about it, push it aside, move on with your life." Maybe this is why I had never reached out to any of my fellow hostages, despite what they meant to me during that time. Before the internet it would have been difficult to find them—I had only old phone numbers—but in recent years, I could have searched. It might have been hard to locate women whose names had changed after marriage, as mine had. But I hadn't tried. Maybe it was part of hiding the experience. Or maybe, it was that my travels and research had taken me to faraway places. If I had spoken to other hostages, we would have reflected on the experience we'd shared. I had chosen not to look back.

I'd taken our family advice to an extreme: I'd hidden and not spoken about a person—my brother, Joel—most of my life, so it wasn't that difficult to bury a story like the hijacking. But I paid the cost of carrying my own burdens silently. There's a loneliness to keeping trauma locked inside, in a faraway country no one else can visit. I've learned that telling my story to others can be healing both for myself and for others who carry hidden trauma.

Not acknowledging the emotional pain that I experienced, first in my family and later from my hijacking, became a pattern. A path of avoidance, of diminishing my feelings, of not connecting with them fully. I've had to accept that I've experienced trauma, that I'm a trauma survivor. I never thought of myself that way, though I'm not sure why. Perhaps we simply didn't have the language for it at the time, and by the time we did, enough time had passed that I didn't make the connection.

Maybe it didn't fit with my identity as a resilient person who has been able to move on. My resilience was a protective armor, allowing me to go back into the world without ever addressing what happened. To begin to heal, I've had to acknowledge the submerged trauma. Now I embrace both roles—being a survivor and being resilient—and see the connection between them. Researchers in the field of post-traumatic growth find that people can *benefit* from trauma by gaining a new appreciation for their strengths and coping abilities. This has been true for me. Having a better understanding of myself and accepting my resilience gives me confidence in the face of new challenges.

Now that I've been talking openly about being a hostage, I've been surprised by people's interest and the many questions they have about my experience. Often, people tell me I'm brave for traveling the world and living for extended periods in so many countries. But I have never felt brave. People I've lived with in South and Southeast Asia seem a lot braver than I am, given how they cope with the precarity and uncertainty that constantly face them. As an anthropologist, I've documented the life stories of oppressed and economically impoverished people who struggle daily to feed their families and seek necessary medical care. Their narratives have helped me recognize how fortunate I am. My own trauma seems distant and small in comparison to the struggles of their everyday lives. Yet it is not.

To honor my experience as a hostage, I immersed myself in writing, which became a therapeutic process. As I pulled on the threads of memory, new details revealed themselves, often accompanied by tears. Tissues lay scattered on my desk, testaments to buried emotions that had finally surfaced.

Penning this book has been a cleansing process, a dredging up, and a letting go. I still cry, but much less frequently. And now when my tears stop flowing, I'm able to leave the sad memories and move on with my day. That seems like progress.

EPILOGUE

One day while surfing the internet, I stumbled upon a book, *Terror in Black September: The First Eyewitness Account of the Infamous 1970 Hijackings*, published in 2008. The book was written by a fellow hostage, David Raab. I emailed him, suggesting we should talk. In the more than four decades since the hijacking, this would be my first time speaking with another hostage.

After his return from Jordan, David had given numerous talks at Jewish organizations about his experience as a hostage. A college student at the time, he enjoyed talking about it although he remained fearful of traveling again by plane. To allay his fears, he finally booked a ticket to Tel Aviv and flew back to New York on the same TWA flight we had been on when the plane was hijacked. This strategy worked. It reminded me of Mark's advice—to go back into the world and travel, lest I become immobilized forever.

"Have you kept in touch with other hostages?" I asked. "Do you know what happened to Rachel?"

"She lives near me in New Jersey," he replied. "I think she didn't talk much about the hijacking. When I was writing my book, I traveled to Jordan and visited the place we were held in Amman. An old man came out—who I did not know—and asked me about the young woman who spoke Arabic—he remembered her. I guess people in the community had talked about her. When I got home, I shared the story with Rachel. I think she started talking more about the experience after that."

"What about Bob, Mike, and Ben?" I asked, suddenly eager to know more.

"Well, I've been in touch with Ben's son because by the time I reached out to his family, Ben had died of cancer."

"I'm so sorry to hear that he passed." I took a moment to mull over this sad news. "Ben was such an upbeat guy, so funny and caring—that's how I'll always remember him. He helped us get through the hard times with his positive spirit."

"I know, that's how I feel too," David agreed.

"And Bob? We sat next to each other on the flight out of Tel Aviv. Such a nice guy. He explained what was going on when I didn't have a clue."

"Yup, he was a good guy. I tried to get hold of him but couldn't. I couldn't find Mike either. You know, people scattered."

"It's amazing that you kept in touch with people and know what's happened to so many of us, David."

"Thanks. My family—all five of us who were on the plane—celebrate the day of our return home every year. We live in Israel part of the year. My children know the story of the hijacking and my grandkids do, too. I still think about it almost every day. Something comes up and I remember."

David and I hadn't talked for forty years, and yet we shared a life-changing event that remained vivid for both of us. After our call, he sent me a signed copy of his book, which I read with great interest. He'd written a comprehensive, well-researched historical record that also included personal memories. His memories mostly resonated with my own.

In the days and weeks that followed, I thought about what it might have been like to talk openly about the hijacking right after it happened. Would it have been an easier path for me to have spoken about it early on, rather than having it bottled up inside me for years? But there was no gain in looking back or engaging in "what if" thinking; that's who I was then—and remained for many years.

During the COVID-19 pandemic, in the summer of 2020, David emailed that he was organizing a fifty-year reunion on Zoom for TWA passengers. The reunion was planned for September 6th, the day the plane had been hijacked. Despite my excitement, I wondered how it would feel to reconnect with other hostages.

David requested that before the reunion each participant prepare a short video clip introducing themselves and sharing where they lived and something about their current work and family life. Together, we decided to ask people to recall their most poignant memory from the hijacking and say how the experience affected their lives.

A few days before the reunion, I received a link to the videos that others had sent. I was teary when I saw the other women I had been with in the apartment, Rachel, Shoshana, and Susan, now almost seventy years old. I felt a bond that had survived fifty years. Though I might not have recognized them if we passed on the street, their affect and presentation on their videos reminded me of their younger selves. Rachel was thoughtful and self-composed, Shoshana was still her quirky, joking self, and Susan appeared a bit reserved and articulate.

I tried to locate Bob and Mike to tell them about the reunion and was sad to discover that both had died. I wished I had reached out to them when I could have. I texted Mike's son and invited him to participate in the reunion, but he chose not to.

On the morning of the Zoom, I woke early, my mind buzzing, my stomach busy with butterflies. I laid out my yoga mat to calm myself by stretching my arms toward the sky and bowing to my feet. Three sun salutations focused and grounded me. I included camel and rabbit poses in honor of the emotional release about the hijacking they had inspired.

Forty people from the United States and Israel joined the reunion call. Everyone reintroduced themselves briefly, mentioning how old they were on the plane, how long they were held, and where they were in life today.

About a quarter of those at the reunion had made Aliyah to Israel in the years following the hijacking. *Aliyah* literally means to ascend or go up and refers to the immigration of Jews to Israel. Some of those who now lived in Israel expressed a sentiment of having triumphed over the PFLP. As one ex-hostage explained: "The PFLP wanted us out of Israel, but I'm here to stay with my family!" Shoshana was there among them, and she had chosen to make Aliyah on the anniversary of the hijacking. "We're still here," she quipped. "They wanted us gone but we've come back."

Some interpreted the hijacking as part of God's plan, "that we had been saved for a purpose," to return and repopulate Israel. I was reminded of God's commandment to the Jewish people, *pru u'rvu*, be fruitful and multiply. The former hostages who had settled in Israel had obeyed this commandment. Proud grandparents on the reunion call shared that they had large families, which included twenty and even thirty grandchildren, all living in Israel. By comparison, my own family, two children and two grandchildren, seemed minuscule.

Most of the people on the Zoom had been released after six days and had not been there during the civil war, but the hijacking remained significant in their lives. Several people said that as adults, they suffered with every hostage crisis that occurred, regardless of where it was in the world. One woman remarked that memories of the hijacking remain vivid, even as she struggles to remember what happened the previous day. Many expressed that our coming home alive was a miracle and if the hijacking had occurred a few years later, we would have been killed—even beheaded.

Several others reported that they had chosen not to talk about the hijacking, saying it was a fraught memory that could be overwhelming if brought to the surface during conversation. Even those who had been held for six days or less described triggers that could dredge up their fears and memories. On the other hand, some people shared that they often related the story of the hijacking when they were in group settings, exuding a sense of pride they had survived.

Overall, there was a tremendous appreciation for David for organizing the reunion and bringing us together. Though the hijacking had occurred fifty years earlier, the intensity of our memories had not faded. It was meaningful for me to listen to others' memories of the hijacking and to share mine with others. Despite our many differences, we were all connected, each etched by the event in our own way.

The impact of the hijacking seemed to depend, at least in part, on how old a person was at that time. Children who were too young to comprehend the gravity and danger of the situation appeared to have suffered little residual trauma. Perhaps that is to be expected. Some did not try to understand the experience until they were much older. Martha Hodes, for example, was twelve years old and traveling only with her fourteen-year-old sister on the plane; the girls were held for six days. I remembered them from the plane, but they had not joined us in our kids' "camp." For most of her life, Martha suppressed the memory of the hijacking. Then, after 9/11, faint memories and questions arose. A professional historian, Martha pored over archival accounts, read journals, and conducted interviews to write *My Hijacking: A Personal History of Forgetting and Remembering*. It is intriguing that both of us felt the need to explore the hijacking after so many years.

Among young adults like me, the aftereffects appeared to be more complex and differed by individual. The lasting impact of the hijacking appeared to be most universally painful for older people—Holocaust survivors and parents traveling with children—who understood the peril of the hijacking from the first moment.

Since the hijacking, I have never returned to Israel or Jordan, but as I was writing this memoir, I decided it was finally time to go. Unfortunately, I had to cancel my plans because of the pandemic, and more recently because of the ongoing fighting in Israel. But we have each other's emails, and since the hostage crisis in Gaza, there has been frequent communication among our own hostage group, especially when those who had been held for over fifteen months were finally released. Seeing these televised moments brings back intense memories of our own release.

Of late, I have been asked how I feel about the current Israeli–Palestinian crisis. After two years of brutal warfare, I have come to believe, along with many Jewish Americans, that Israeli attacks on Gaza have gone on for far too long. This humanitarian crisis needs to end, and all the remaining deceased hostages in Gaza need to be returned to their families for burial. While I understand the need for Israelis to ensure their safety, I also recognize the need of the Palestinian people to be peacefully settled on land they can call their own. Our hijacking was an early attempt for global recognition of their liminal status. Sadly, these violent attempts will no doubt continue until a peaceful resolution is finally achieved in the region.

ACKNOWLEDGMENTS

Penning this book required introspection and memory-dredging—had I understood just how much it would take, I might not have begun. I was fortunate to have people in my life who were interested in a story I had not yet told, who provided support throughout my journey.

Special thanks and a debt of gratitude to my dear friend Penelope Jacks, who read chapters early on and provided honest and insightful feedback and encouragement that contributed to moving the book forward. She believed in the book even in its earliest stages.

Thanks to the many readers and friends who offered comments and suggestions on earlier drafts: Liz Cartwright, Denise Coyne, Amy Lederman, Marge Mather, Carolyn Nordstrom, Bari Ross, David Schachter, Karen Spiegel, Benedict Tisa, Vinitha, Melanie Wallendorf, and Heidi Yamaguchi. Many thanks to Nicole Taylor, who was patient and understanding as I toggled between the memoir and a book on social media we were cowriting at the time.

As a recovering academic, I had a lot to learn about writing a memoir. Along the path of Zoom classes and workshops, I found Allison K. Williams and Dinty Moore, seasoned writing teachers whose workshops and retreats expanded my understanding of what it takes to write and revise a memoir. Many thanks also to writing coach and teacher Theo Nestor. Editor extraordinaire Jessica Strawser provided valuable edits and guidance for going deeper that greatly enhanced the readability of the book.

My writing circle with Marjie Alonso, Sana Fayyaz, and Charlotte Wilkins has miraculously managed to keep me laughing through the vicissitudes of writing. Their edits and suggestions for my writing have been especially useful. And a special shoutout to fellow writer and friend Rebecca Morrison, who continues to be upbeat and generous in sharing her knowledge of the publication process.

Heartfelt appreciation to all my family members who listened to my story and read early drafts, asked questions, and offered suggestions. My sons, Simeon Nichter and Brandon Nichter, my daughter-in-law, Maysa Eissa Nichter, my one and only sister, Deborah Riverbend, and her son, Jon Givner, were all enthusiastic and encouraging from the beginning.

Special thanks to David Raab, author of *Terror in Black September*, whose book triggered many memories of the hostage journey we shared. I appreciate his continued efforts to keep former hostages in touch with one another.

This book would not have found the right home if it were not for my agent, Murray Weiss, at Catalyst Literary Management. Taylor Gilreath, my editor at Potomac Books, and Kayla Moslander have been a pleasure to work with throughout the process, providing answers to my many questions along the path of publication. Many thanks also to my careful and thoughtful copyeditor, Stephanie Marshall Ward.

And, finally, forever thanks to Mark Nichter, who cared for me when I first returned to college after the hijacking, through the times the experience haunted me and begged to be told, and throughout the writing of this book. Our many discussions over the years in remote corners of the globe helped me explore memories from that time and reflect on the impact of being a hostage on my life.

OTHER WORKS BY MIMI NICHTER

A Filtered Life: Social Media on a College Campus (with Nicole Taylor)

Lighting Up: The Rise of Social Smoking on College Campuses

Fat Talk: What Girls and Their Parents Say about Dieting

Anthropology and International Health: Asian Case Studies (with Mark Nichter)

www.ingramcontent.com/pod-product-compliance
Lightning Source LLC
Chambersburg PA
CBHW021031100126
37952CB00005B/20

* 9 7 8 1 6 4 0 1 2 6 8 4 8 *